Spirit of the Road:

Road:

The Life of an American Trucker

...and his cat

2nd Edition
Revised and Expanded

Rick L. Huffman

ISBN-13: 978-1492252368
ISBN-10: 1492252360

To protect the privacy of some who have shared stories and adventures with the author, some details and names have been changed.

CMV Publications

For Tonie;

And for all the men and women who sacrifice more than most will ever know to deliver freight across the nation.

A travelogue

Contents

Foreword to the 2nd Edition *9*

Introduction *11*

Trucking School *14*

Training with Ringo *22*

The First Delivery *25*

Week 1: Coon Dogs and the Lizard Man *28*

Week 2: Accident on I-85 ....*32*

Week 3: School of Hard Knocks *36*

Week 4: Frostproof Ladders and   Hooterville *38*

Week 5: Slip Sliding Away *41*

Week 6: French Lick and the Forest *43*

Detour: Trucking in a Winter Blunderland *45*

Week 7: Bear Creek, Egypt, and Kitty *51*

Week 8: Mountain Man *53*

Week 9: Trucking, Fort Rucker, and Einstein *58*

Week 10: Loafers and Burmese Chickens *62*

Week 11: Buckets of Mud *65*

Week 12: A Smoke Tarp, The Broken Yolk, and Jack Daniels ..*67*

Detour: A View from the Cab *71*

Week 13: Take this job and... ....*78*

Week 14 and 15: Greener Pastures *80*

Week 16: Orientation, Merlin, and a Plumbing Misfortune *82*

Week 17 and 18: Tragedy in Cross Timbers *89*

Detour: Drivers versus Dispatchers? *95*

Week 19: Life with Brian *99*

Week 20 and 21: No Trucks Allowed!..................*101*

Week 23: Avian Droppings *109*

Week 24: Low Times in High Springs..................*113*

Detour: Fitness, Hygiene, and Diet on the Road..................*117*

Week 25: Driver "Appreciation" *121*

Week 26: Frozen Orange Juice and Dispatcher Bob.............*123*

Week 27: "Shagged" again! *126*

Week 28: Here Kitty, Kitty *128*

Week 29: Goodbye Dispatcher Bob......................*130*

Week 30: A Kansas Moon *133*

Detour: Lot Lizards *137*

Week 31: A Loose Nut in Texas..........................*140*

Week 32: El Paso, Pecos, and a Cracked Radiator *144*

Week 33: The Nudist Camp and a Chicago Scrape...............*147*

Week 34: I Ain't Got No Quarters! *151*

Week 35: Eat More Possum *156*

Week 36: Is that alligator staring at me?............*159*

Detour: Spirituality on the Road *162*

Week 37 and 38: Kitty Foams at the Mouth.........*166*

Week 39: Roadside Emergency and a Walmart Bag.............*170*

Week 40: Georgia Chicken Coop *174*

Week 41: Detroit, Kalamazoo, and Buffalo Commons..........*178*

Week 42: RC Cola and Moon Pie *183*

Detour: The Lonely Road *187*

Week 43: Macon Whoopee *191*

8

Week 44: Jersey Manners and the Flopeye Fish Festival.......194

Week 45: Silly Four-Wheelers and Squeaky Cheese..............198

Week 46: Darth Vader and the World's Largest Truck Stop..200

Week 47: Toad Suck Park and Beer Nuts.............................204

Week 48: Imprisoned Kitty and Grandma Moses 208

Detour: The Image of Truckers 212

Week 49 and 50: Searching for Elvis 217

Week 51: Frigid in Fridley 222

Week 52: Reflections 225

Afterword 228

In Memoriam 231

Endnotes 239

Foreword to the 2nd Edition

First of all, I'd like to thank you for checking out my book. When I sat down in January of 2008 to begin the arduous task of piecing together my scribblings from the road into some semblance of coherency, I never knew I'd still be honing the edges of *Spirit of the Road* some seven years later. It has been a labor of both love and travail that has allowed me to cultivate my lifelong ambition to be a writer into reality. It has also pushed me to tackle other writing projects as I strive to grow and improve…which brings me to the purpose of a second edition.

The reasons for a second edition are twofold. First, after reading the manuscript again over a year later, I saw many opportunities to enhance, update, and improve the work. The passage of time affords a more objective eye, and the gift of additional experience affords a more discerning one. I concluded that enough change was warranted to justify a second edition. As I continue to evolve as a writer, I remain committed to producing the best work of which I am capable. I am humbled and grateful each time someone is kind enough to buy my book.

The second reason is because Kitty passed away in the summer of 2014, and it just seemed appropriate to make an update to that end since Kitty played a vital role in this story. I have included a heartfelt memorial to Kitty at the end of this edition.

Once again, I'd like to thank everyone who has been gracious enough to support me in my writing endeavors as I work toward completing my first novel. It is the most difficult and challenging work I've ever done, but it is also the most gratifying. In saying this, I would be remiss not to thank Tonie, the wonderful woman in my life whose unwavering faith and support give me the strength, courage, and confidence that I could have never found on my own.

I invite you to join me on a unique and life-changing journey as Kitty and I discover the surprising, uplifting, daunting, insufferable, frightening, and sometimes hilarious spirit of the road. I hope that you'll be entertained and informed as you are along for the ride but, above all, I hope you'll have fun.

Rick L. Huffman

February, 2015

Introduction

In October of 2005, I enrolled in an Alabama Commercial Driving School and began a new adventure that was invigorating, intimidating and, at times, even infuriating. I was probably one of the most unlikely candidates to become a truck driver that the world has ever seen. Not only had I worked in a sedentary job for the past 20 years, I had never driven anything larger than a U-Haul. To be sure, my skills at maneuvering any vehicle bigger than a Ford Focus left a lot to be desired. I once attempted to back a U-Haul to the door of my former girlfriend's apartment. She finally grew weary of observing my struggle and offered to take over. While I can't swear to it, I think that I could literally feel my testosterone level depleting as she deftly maneuvered the truck exactly where it needed to be.

Meanwhile, I had spent the past 20 years of my life working in television broadcasting in various roles. While it had been exciting and challenging at first, the years had eroded my role into a thankless and suffocating rut. As an added garnish, fate had also grabbed my personal life by the nape of the neck and dunked it into the crapper for a humiliating "swirly." I seriously needed a change…a new experience. I can only chalk it up to chance that I ran across one of those *Big Trucks Mean Big Bucks* ads in the Sunday paper and, unlike the dozens of other times that I'd seen (and ignored) them, it caught my eye this time. If a significant change was what I needed, this certainly seemed to be the ticket.

In the following pages, I will share the experiences from my first year on the road. This story runs the gambit from a wide-eyed rookie in CDL School to the eventual embracing of a new lifestyle at a dusty little truck stop in Crab Orchard, Tennessee. My loyal traveling cat began riding with me at the start of my fourth solo week on the road, and she would be with me for the remainder of my travels. In 1995, an abandoned kitten showed up on the doorstep of my Huntsville, Alabama apartment making an appeal for food. After weeks of feeding the little kitten, I finally took her to the vet to bring her to full health and claimed her as my own. Over the next decade, the little cat would accompany me through the peaks and valleys of life until we ended up rolling across the country together in an 18-wheeler. My road adventures would not be complete without Kitty at my side.

There are over 3.4 million long-distance truck drivers in the United States and millions more in local delivery operations. Motorists share the highway with them every day yet, little is known about the lifestyle of a long-haul trucker outside of the inner sanctum of the trucking industry. Hollywood paints truckers as uneducated southern rednecks who are heavily adorned in denim and flannel. Through his tobacco-stained teeth, he necessarily hits on every woman he sees while hiding his wedding ring.

In truth, trucking attracts people as diverse as the aforementioned stereotype to former doctors, CEO's, bankers, and engineers. I even met a MENSA member with a reefer in tow at a Kentucky truck stop. The diversity among truckers is just as great as in any other profession. You never know what stories hide beneath the grimy visor of a truck driver...or *who* hides beneath it.

The trucking industry is a rapidly evolving entity and, as I write this today, it has changed much since I first set foot inside that old flattop Mack with my first driver trainer. Whether it has evolved for the better is debatable and differing opinions are sure to be found depending on who you ask. In 2005, GPS systems exclusively made for truck drivers were not readily available for purchase. Some drivers used mapping software on a laptop or MapQuest, but most drivers still used a road atlas and written or verbal directions that were accurate only if you were lucky on that day. The continual piling on of more and more DOT regulations, the advent of electronic logs, and new safety programs that began with CSA 2010 keeps the trucking industry in a state of constant flux.

I seek neither to champion the causes of truckers nor to disparage the trucking industry. The possible occurrence of either is merely coincidental to the telling of the story. I make no claim that my view is the correct one or that my opinion reflects that of all truckers. This is simply an account from one driver's perspective, and I tell it from the viewpoint of a company driver. The only guarantee I make is that the story will be told with honesty and from a singular perspective.

It is said that everyone has a story to tell. This is the story an American trucker…and his cat.

Rick L. Huffman – June, 2013

Trucking School

The faint aroma of cheap carpet deodorizer provided but a thin veil to the underlying stink of old cigarette smoke which clung to everything in the meager motel room like a blood-engorged tick. The anxious sounds of the medical staff in a makeshift ER erupted from the small television set as Hawkeye and Trapper John raced to mend wounded soldiers in a *MASH* rerun. The offensive smell and the noise from the television were in the back of my mind as I watched traffic zoom north and south on Interstate 65 from my motel room window in Priceville, Alabama. Tomorrow would be the first day of CDL School where my introduction to the world of long haul trucking would begin. I knew my life was about to change abruptly.

To say that I knew nothing of trucking would be putting it mildly. To be sure, my understanding of operating a big rig was proportionately equal to my understanding of quantum physics. I had no idea what to expect on the first day of trucking school, but I did suspect that this new chapter of my life would not be boring. I could not have been more right.

I was anxious on Monday morning as I entered the unremarkable brick building that would serve as my training headquarters for the next three weeks. A worn American flag and an Alabama state flag whipped hastily in the breeze. A thick cloud of dust swirled up from the large dirt lot in back of the school where a row of about a dozen eighteen-wheelers patiently awaited their new occupants.

As the routine indoctrination procedures of the first day progressed, I slowly became familiar with some of the other students. The most striking revelation was that the students came from all walks of life and from wildly varied backgrounds. The Hollywood stereotype of the dim-witted redneck trucker with a bulging cheek of chewing tobacco was already being challenged. As the morning progressed, some of the students shared their stories with one another and I formed a bond with Alan, a former engineer.

Alan was a transplant from England and, although he had lived in the United States for sixteen years, his Cockney accent remained undiminished. As I would later discover, his accent became even more pronounced when he was aggravated or nervous, sometimes to the point where I had trouble understanding him. Alan was laid off from his engineering job and, at 54; he had experienced the frustration and despair of searching for new employment in competition with much younger candidates. Like me, Alan had a lot riding on the success of this new gamble.

Alan and I were often kept amused by the antics of Steve, who was the biggest comedian of all the students, both literally and figuratively. The jovial and inviting personality of this former football player belied his imposing ebony frame.

"Why did 18 truckers go to a movie together?" asks Steve with a mischievous grin.

"I don't know," we reply.

"Because it said under 17 not admitted," answers Steve with an enormous roar of laughter.

I never saw Steve without his trademark perpetual smile. He was always fun to be around and he, usually, kept everyone laughing, especially Ray.

Ray was a foil to Steve as his rail-thin form barely lifted him to the height of Steve's armpit even with the aid of cowboy boots. Despite the slightness of Steve's wee antithesis, Ray proved to be one of the ablest students in the class.

Regardless of the varied personalities, everyone here had at least one thing in common. Each person sought a better life for himself or, he wanted to get his life back on track from a prior misfortune. It came as no surprise when camaraderie quickly developed among most of us.

The indoctrination procedures and physicals consumed all of the morning, and then it was time to begin classroom studies. Classroom training during the first week would prepare us for the written portion of the CDL test, and the next two weeks would introduce road training.

The classroom instructor was a rotund middle-aged fellow named Ron. Ron immediately conveyed an air of confidence despite a distracting habit of constantly rubbing his goatee. He wiped at it with urgency, as if he were trying to remove an erroneous splash of pea soup from his chin. However, it soon became apparent that Ron had probably forgotten more about trucking than most of us would ever know. Thanks to his expertise, most of the fifteen students passed the written exam on the first attempt. Eventually, everyone passed. Now, it was time to drive the trucks. Oh boy...

Alan and I bantered nervously in the crisp morning air of the big day. White asters at the edge of the training yard danced to and fro in the fresh morning breeze as the new day cast its first light. Both of us were nervous, yet excited about the new challenge before us as we anxiously awaited the arrival of the instructor. We would spend the first couple of days in the yard learning straight-line backing and 45-degree angle backing.

The instructor entered the yard as the sun peeked over the east horizon and waved for us to join him at the row of trucks in the yard. The rank of ancient long-nosed Freightliners and dilapidated Volvos brought to mind an image of old battle-scarred warriors who should be resting in retirement, but have been recalled to active duty to form one final phalanx.

The instructor's name was James, who was a little younger than Ron, but whose shoulders were slightly hunched as if he'd been carrying a cinder block before arriving. He had a cookie duster mustache and spoke in a nasal monotone, which inspired me to gulp my coffee with increased urgency. James, as we soon discovered, had a penchant for talking about women's breasts. He didn't just talk about them—he analyzed them: the shape, the size, the feel, the texture, the rating system, the color, the roundness of the areola, the smoothness, the pear-shaped ones, the apple-shaped ones...well, you get the picture. At first, the mammary musings of James were amusing but, after a time, it began to get a little creepy. He wore his obsession with "ogling the oompahs" like a sandwich board. While I freely admit my appreciation for female breasts, they are rarely exposed as a topic in one of my regular conversations. James, however, spoke of breasts as if he were casually talking about the weather. Nevertheless, James was our instructor now, and I fervently hoped that he had more knowledge to bestow upon us than the most plausible route to "Wapbapaloobop World" in Las Vegas.

After half an hour of verbal instructions, James climbed into a timeworn Volvo laced with rust and fired it up. The quavering roar of the diesel engine drowned out the sounds of morning as it declared itself the ruler of its antediluvian domain. Even Steve was dwarfed standing next to the sputtering giant. James maneuvered the wheezing vehicle between two rows of orange cones and told us that we'd be learning straight-line backing today. He then pointed directly at me and asked for my name.

"Rick," I answered.

"Okay Rick," grinned James, "you're first—jump in!"

I climbed up into the shuddering vehicle with trepidation while some of the students wished me good luck, and others wagered on how many orange cones I'd crush. James emerged at the window and shouted a reminder at me over the noise of the gravelly engine.

"Steer into your trouble… if the trailer goes right—steer right, if the trailer goes left—steer left."

With that, he climbed down from the vehicle and left me to the task. The old Volvo now shook with authority as if it were a rodeo bull eager to dismount me in less than eight seconds. The mirrors vibrated so violently that I couldn't even see the cones; they appeared as orange blurs.

I took a deep breath and began my backward trek. Amazingly, I managed to negotiate the 100-yard course without hitting any cones, but it didn't take long to discover that this was trickier than it seemed. Another hundred yards and there's no doubt that I would have killed some cones. Over the next few days, I practiced and gained confidence. Then, I was introduced to the bane of my existence: 45-degree angle backing.

Almost everyone is abysmal at 45-degree angle backing to start, and I was no exception. Alan even resorted to mathematical equations to crack this puzzle, but it didn't seem to help either of us. As we pondered the mysteries of this elusive skill, another student approached us to provide unsolicited mentoring. I cannot recall his name, so I'll just call him *Douchebag*. In addition to vacant green eyes, greasy brown hair, and a set of British teeth that probably made Alan homesick, Douchebag possessed a conviction of his mastery of 45-degree angle backing. Since the beginning of the school, Douchebag leaped at every chance to offer unwelcome insight to both students and instructors. By this time, most of the students attempted to avoid his tutelage, viewing him as more pest than mentor.

In truth, backing a big truck is more art than science. The only way to improve is through sheer repetition. Unfortunately, there was a limited amount of time and opportunities to practice before our road test. Concern arose among many of the students. We didn't see how we'd possibly be ready in time.

Enter Pat.

Pat was another yard instructor; a petite middle-aged lady with closely cropped blonde hair and a forceful presence. She was a seasoned veteran of the road, having traveled many miles with a loyal canine companion named Zip Code.

"I named him that because he's been in every zip code," explained Pat.

She said the course in the yard was set up exactly the same way it would be for the test. Then, she pulled a Joe Namath moment out of her hat:

"We've done this week in and week out with hundreds of students, and I guarantee I'll have you ready for your test."

She spoke with such confidence that I didn't write her words off as bluster—I believed her. True to her word, she showed us tricks that yielded immediate results. The skills she taught us wouldn't have helped a bit at the dock of a crowded shipper, but they helped immensely in learning to get the trailer between the cones on this course.

This brings up a point. A two or three-week trucking school is, essentially, a boot camp toward getting a CDL. Given the short time frame, the student is crammed with the essential knowledge to pass the test...period. There is no time to perfect or hone any of the basic skills. Make no mistake; a student fresh out of CDL School is **NOT** prepared to be on the road in an eighteen-wheeler. That is why, upon being hired by his first company, a new driver will spend, on average, six to eight weeks with a driver trainer before going solo. The role of a CDL school is to whip a student into shape to pass the CDL test. That's it.

In the meantime, we had been going out in groups of four with other instructors to drive on a low-traffic route in Decatur, Alabama to learn how to shift through the 10 gears. Donny was the first instructor to endure the comedy of errors from my group. Donny was a laid-back country boy with rugged features, for whom sitting at the helm of an eighteen-wheeler seemed as natural to him as putting on his pants in the morning. Donny was as cool as a cucumber and remained supportive despite our beginner mistakes. For the first couple of days, there was more grinding taking place in those trucks than in a Starbucks factory.

Another instructor I rode with was Rick, a compact and vigorous black man. He possessed the hyperactive energy of a sugar-buzzed motivational speaker who had just swum fifty laps in a pool filled with coffee and Red Bull. Rick earned the nickname of "Boom Boom" because, his method of instruction for the proper time to shift gears was:

"Okay, get ready—BOOM! Get ready—BOOM!"

Boom Boom relayed countless road stories to us, and his irrepressible personality made him the most entertaining of the instructors.

Finally, the time to take the road test arrived. We would go, in small groups, to the testing facility in Hartselle, Alabama over the next five days. I would test on the second day, and Alan would test on the fourth. Everyone was nervous, so I guess Alan just needed a laugh when he approached Douchebag and asked, "Do you think you're going to pass?"

"I KNOW I'm going to pass!" boasted Douchebag proudly.

Douchebag failed on his first two attempts.

The test consisted of four parts: first, the student would provide a verbal commentary of an inspection of the truck and trailer. Next would be straight-line backing followed by 45-degree angle backing and, finally, driving on the road with the evaluating officer.

On my test day, the diminutive Ray and another student named Jerome accompanied me. Jerome was missing most of his front teeth, but that didn't stop him from flashing an endearing smile. The poignant circumstances leading Jerome to CDL school had me, along with everyone else, in his corner rooting for him. The scuttlebutt among the instructors, however, didn't give him a snowball's chance in hell of passing. On this day, Jerome's smile was missing and he was nervous to the point of trembling. It helped to relieve some of my tension as I offered encouragement to him as best I could.

Ray was the first to test and despite being barely big enough to reach the pedals, he passed on the first attempt. Next was Jerome. Pat was the instructor who had accompanied us and she didn't seem optimistic. Jerome, however, rose to the occasion and shocked everyone. He got what held up to be the highest score of anyone in the class.

"I didn't see that coming," is all Pat could say.

Now it was my turn. We were two for two today, and I certainly wanted to keep the streak intact. I breezed through the inspection because Alan and I had unmercifully drilled each other on this until we had it down cold. Straight-line backing didn't prove to be a problem either. Then, it was time for the dreaded 45-degree angle backing. After my heart had skipped a few beats, I set up the way Pat had showed us, and I slowly maneuvered the trailer between the cones. It was perfection! I was dead center perfect! My confidence soared as I got out marveling at my trailer which sat neatly across the first chalk line. It was already a passing grade! However, I thought that I could back a little closer to the rear cone to improve my score. I returned to the driver's seat and backed up just a little. Then I rushed out to observe my mastery, knowing that I'd just sent my score into the stratosphere.

My life flashed before my eyes in horror as I found the rearmost cone lying horizontal as if it were a bowling pin toppled with a Brunswick from the hand of Walter Ray Williams Jr. I looked at the officer with an imploring appeal but, as the fallen cone lay there like a slug, he had no choice but to fail me.

I was devastated. I moped to the curb and sat down with my head in my hands. Our roles reversed, Jerome came over to offer encouragement. I was pissed off at myself because my ego had caused me to fail. I'd just been trying to run up the score. I deserved to fail, and I knew it. Jerome didn't allow me to feel sorry for myself for long though.

"Git up and go take that Muthafucka again!" he insisted.

"I know you can do it an' I'm gone kick yo' Muthafuckin ass if you don't go take that Muthafucka again!"

His words were blunt, straightforward, and to the point. I decided to go and take that Muthafucka again.

This time, I collected myself and left my ego at the door. I backed the trailer between the cones and got out three or four times to assess my progress. When the rear of the trailer was across the first passing line, I looked at the officer and asked, "Is that passing?"

He could not conceal an amused grin when he said, "Yeah, that's passing. Do you want to go for a higher score?"

"No, sir!" I stated with conviction.

The road test went well and, after the emotional roller coaster ride of today, I could rest easy now—I had passed.

The majority of the class did not pass on the first attempt. Even Alan had to take a second stab at it. Nevertheless, everyone eventually got a CDL—even Douchebag. I was going to miss many of these guys, especially Alan, but it was now time to find my first trucking job. I decided to take my first job with a flatbed company out of Savannah, Georgia. I'd be running southeast regional and working out of their Bridgeport, Alabama terminal. After going through orientation in Savannah, taking a physical and signing a ton of paperwork, I met my trainer—and Ringo was his name-o.

Training with Ringo

Ringo was an imposing grizzly bear of a man with a thick, gray-flecked forest of a beard and, despite his thinning hair, he continued to grow steely, shoulder-length locks. He looked like an oversized caricature of Hank Williams Jr. The piercing resonance of Ringo's thunderous baritone voice implied that he probably did not own any wine glasses.

When he arrived to pick me up in the red, white and blue Mack, I loaded my gear into the truck in anxious anticipation of my first week on the road. As I began to settle in, I observed, in horror, only one sleeper berth. Did they expect us to share? Having recently seen the movie *Brokeback Mountain*, my butt cheeks instinctively tightened and my anus puckered into an impenetrable fortress. Ringo sensed my panic and released a powerful belly laugh.

"The company's gonna give us a condo next week," he explained between chuckles. "We're stuck in this flat top this week so, we'll just have to do the best we can. You can have the sleeper the first couple of nights 'till you get settled."

I heaved a sigh of relief and Ringo continued to chortle for the next few miles. Ringo had recently returned to the company after spending a year driving for a private owner. I was his first trainee. This would be a new experience for both of us.

Over the next six weeks, we traversed the southeast together and Ringo displayed patience and understanding that belied his, sometimes, brash personality. Ringo could be described as many things, but boring is not among them. He regaled me with road stories and death-defying tales from his youth during our six weeks together. I never knew, with certainty, how much truth these stories contained but, oftentimes, an allegorical truth is just as enlightening as a literal one. Ringo was, without question, a bard of the open road. He also had a habit of bringing interrogative closure to many of his observations with the query, "You know what I mean?" I didn't give it much thought to begin with but, after a time, I started to wonder if Ringo were channeling the ghost of the late Jim Varney. To his credit, however, he did find time to provide me with training between yarns.

Since we were running southeast regional, we would get to go home on weekends. However, I would soon discover that the company's idea of a "weekend" was often displayed by getting the driver home late Friday evening and then, dispatching him on a load that required him to leave on Sunday morning. The "trucker's weekend" was not something for which I'd been prepared.

The first couple of weeks were hard, because my body was not conditioned to this pace, this type of work, or these long hours. I lost most of the feeling in the tips of my fingers, and I had aches in places where I would have sworn I didn't have places. My former sedentary job was a world away as I wrestled with 130-pound tarps, threw straps, climbed atop towering loads, and stretched bungee cords to secure the tarps. Sometimes, this had to be done in cold, wet, or muddy conditions but, gradually, my body began to adapt to the rigors of its new duties. My road-toughness would not approach the level of Ringo's during the six weeks I rode with him, but I would eventually get it to a standard that I would have formerly thought impossible.

Ringo also introduced me to some places on the map that make a new driver sweat. One such place was the Green River Gorge on I-40 in North Carolina. I had already heard some horror stories pertaining to "The Gorge" and I have, since, seen the aftermath of a rollover while driving through it. However, I came to realize that The Gorge is nothing to fear so long as it is approached with respect and common sense. Accidents happen there because, quite simply, some drivers go through it too fast.

I was, nonetheless, a bit tense the first time I descended Monteagle in Tennessee. I would later view Monteagle as little more than a bump in the road after traveling through the Rockies, but I attempt to never have a cavalier attitude toward descending a mountain in a big truck. I have never forgotten the words of Boom Boom in trucking school concerning this:

"You can come down a mountain too slow as many times as you want. You can come down a mountain too fast, once!"

We were taught to use the proper combination of downshifting, tapping the brakes and utilizing Jake brakes to minimize air brake usage. A Jake brake is a mechanism that uses compressed air in the cylinders to slow the vehicle. If you've ever heard a loud and sudden deep guttural growl from a big truck that causes your heart to leap into your throat and your chicken McNuggets to go a'flyin'…that's un-muffled Jake brakes. However, in most places, the law requires them to be muffled nowadays. A driver merely flips a switch to engage them. Still, if you are hauling a 40,000-pound load on a 6% or 7% downgrade— trust me—you'll have to use the air brakes.

I have smelled the acrid odor of smoking brakes more than once while descending a mountain and, each time, I prayed that the smell wasn't emanating from my truck. This is an olfactory experience that every driver fears. I rarely speak for others, but I feel secure in saying that any driver will admit he'd rather whiff a fart brewed from the intestinal fermentation of cheap beer and pickled eggs than to smell his own brakes smoking while descending a mountain.

Ringo and I would sometimes enjoy one another's company and, at other times, merely endure it. Overall, Ringo was an excellent trainer. He provided me with the necessary tools to fly solo and he often gave encouragement when I struggled with my confidence. We remained friends after my training, and later circumstances required me to ask some favors from him to which he eagerly complied. I still think highly of Ringo and wish nothing but the best for him and his family.

Finally, the six weeks of training drew to a conclusion, and it was time for me to be assigned my own truck. I'd pick it up at the company terminal in Mobile, Alabama. I hoped to make Ringo proud by dashing from the starting gate like a well-conditioned thoroughbred. Instead, I stumbled through the chute like a three-legged mare.

The First Delivery

Ringo and I said our goodbyes after spending the night at the Mobile terminal and I was left to pick up my truck, a 2001 flattop Mack with over 600,000 miles on the odometer. It was missing almost all of the necessary equipment and I spent the better part of the morning rounding up my gear.

Finally, I was off on my own. I was nervous, but I was excited too. I had evolved into a safe driver on the road, but my backing skills were still reprehensible. In general, flatbed drivers do less precision backing than dry van drivers because, more often than not, they are loaded and unloaded via forklift out in the open as opposed to in a dock. Precision backing is, nonetheless, required from a flatbed driver too. Ringo once equated my backing skills to "a monkey screwing a football."

My first load assignment had me picking up a load of shingles in Mobile to deliver to Upchurch Building Supply in Greenwood, Mississippi the following day. My message indicated that I had a pre-loaded trailer so, I bob-tailed to the shipper only to discover that my load was at the Mobile terminal. Unbeknownst to me, Ringo and I had spent the night sitting next to my load.

I made a wrong turn on my way back to the terminal and wound up taking an unscheduled tour of Mobile. Eventually, I found my way back and began the arduous task of hooking up to my load and securing it. In training, Ringo and I had worked together with the tarps, straps, and bungee cords but, alone, it seemed as if I were wading through molasses. I was painfully slow, but I wanted to make sure that my load was secure. When I was satisfied, I pulled out to embark on my first solo trip.

By the time I got to Hattiesburg, Mississippi, the heavens had opened up and the rain was pelting down in torrents. It gave me a scare when I stopped at a red light and saw smoke billowing from beneath my trailer. I pulled alongside the road to investigate and decided that this was merely a heat exchange between the rain and the rear trailer tires. I, nonetheless, kept a wary eye behind me as I forged ahead but, as the rain subsided, the steam from the rear tires also lessened. I rolled into a rest area on I-55 near Winona, Mississippi and spent the night there.

I drove to Greenwood the next morning and looked for Upchurch as per my directions. After passing through the entire city, something seemed amiss. I stopped at a convenience store which, luckily, had room for me to turn around and asked a security guard for directions. Upchurch was supposed to be next to Shoney's and, while the guard was unfamiliar with Upchurch, he told me how to get back to Shoney's.

I found Shoney's but still, saw no Upchurch. However, I saw a True Value hardware store so, I pulled in front of it and asked a man, who was going inside, if he knew where Upchurch was.

"This is it," he replied, "The name has just changed."

I had gotten my first taste of trucking company efficiency in providing directions. The difficulties notwithstanding, I had finally located my first customer. All I had to do now was pull around back to be unloaded. Piece of cake!

It was with a combination of dismay and denial when the cartoonish image of a monkey humping a football entered my mind, upon realizing that I had turned down a dead-end alley. The only way to get out would be to do a blindside backing maneuver into the street, with a ditch on both sides. I had promised myself to remain an optimist in my new job, but I suddenly felt that the glass half-full/glass half-empty axiom did not apply to me. I was convinced that life had served me up with a dribble glass!

I was furious with myself for making such a stupid mistake, but I concentrated my efforts on the seemingly impossible task of getting myself out of this mess. My slapstick antics captured the attention of an elderly white-haired man who looked to be in his seventies. As he ambled toward the site of my comical frolic, I could tell by his expression that my driving skills seemed about as natural to him as a supermodel who had just combed her hair with a rock.

"How long have you been driving?" he inquired with a gentle earnestness.

"This is my first delivery," I admitted.

As it turned out, he was the Receiving supervisor at True Value and a 40-year trucking veteran. "I don't mean to tell you your business," he humbly advanced, "but would you like me to help you out?"

I was embarrassed, but I knew I'd gotten in over my head. I politely allowed the friendly old fellow to take over. I'll admit that it dashed my confidence when he maneuvered the truck out of the mess I'd made with precision and ease. Back at the receiving docks, he even had one of his guys to assist me in untarping and unstrapping my load. When the work was complete, I thanked him for his help and apologized for my rookie mistake. He just smiled and said, "Don't worry, it'll get better."

"I hope so," I answered with a sigh.

I didn't know it at the time, but I would meet other kind and endearing people, like this man, in my travels and I would meet others who were not. Nonetheless, I knew that a new adventure lay before me. Despite the blunders of today, my mood was upbeat again. I may have taken a couple of wrong turns and hit a few potholes along the way, but I had successfully made my first delivery. Today had offered the lesson that in trucking, as in life, the path to our destination is rarely a straight one.

Week 1: Coon Dogs and the Lizard Man

The first delivery of my first full solo week was to Simpsonville, South Carolina. This one, thankfully, went very smoothly; the directions were accurate, it was easy to get to, and they unloaded me quickly. This trend, however, would prove to be of the one-in-a-row variety. My next pickup was at International Paper in Newberry, South Carolina.

Newberry, I learned, is home to a witness who reported a sighting of a reptilian monster in 2005 called *The Lizard Man of Scape Ore Swamp*. The Lizard Man is described as being seven feet tall with green, scaly skin and glowing red eyes.[1] The woman in Newberry reported to the police that she had seen two creatures resembling the Lizard Man near her home. The responding officer, in an effort to calm the frightened woman, told her the creatures "just like to check on humans from time to time." While I cannot claim a Lizard Man sighting in Newberry, I still had a bizarre experience of my own there.

My directions said to go 4 miles past the first light in Newberry and the shipper would be on the right. What they should have said was to go **POINT FOUR** (.4) miles after the light. I saw International Paper on the right, just as I zoomed past.

Newberry is a town with narrow streets and many of them are one-way. It was undoubtedly not designed with trucks pulling 48-foot trailers in mind. I finally spotted a road that (almost) appeared to have adequate width to make a left turn, so I gave it a shot. I had to back up a few times and go up on a grassy embankment to avoid taking out a stop sign, but I finally made it back to the interstate and re-entered Newberry to try again.

Déjà vu! I turned into the wrong gate again and the only way out would be to do a blindside backing maneuver into the street similar to the one in Greenwood. I could not believe this! I was starting to feel like God's Hacky sack!

I panicked for a while and looked around, in hopes of seeing another elderly white-haired man. I slowly began to calm myself and then resolved to do what I had to. After a few failed attempts, I managed to get out of there no worse for the wear. While I was fuming at myself for making the same mistake twice, I was happy that I'd been able to clean up my own mess this time. Nevertheless, I determined that a goal worth striving for might be to NOT get into these predicaments in the first place.

I picked up lumber in Newberry, which delivered to Littleville, Alabama. Littleville, mercifully, went very smoothly. On the way to Littleville, I saw a sign for the Coon Dog Cemetery on Highway 72ALT near Tuscumbia, Alabama. At first, I thought it was a joke, but it is a legitimate burial site exclusively for coon dogs.

A man named Key Underwood established the Coon Dog Cemetery in 1937 in tribute to his faithful coon dog, Troop. It is the only cemetery of its kind in the world. Today, more than 185 coon dogs from all across the United States rest in this northwest Alabama memorial.

While I may have had an initial chuckle, I learned that the memory of a loyal coonhound is no joke to an avid coon hunter. When a columnist interviewed Underwood in 1985 and asked why he didn't allow other kinds of dogs to be buried there, his reply was:

"You must not know much about coon hunters and their dogs if you think we would contaminate this burial place with poodles and lap dogs."[2]

From Littleville, I went to Jackson, Tennessee to load steel beams. The massive girders being ferried around by giant magnets appeared quite intimidating. I was glad that I got to stay in the truck the whole time. Afterward, having never tarped steel beams before, I wasn't quite sure how to attack the problem. Fortunately, another company driver out of Savannah spotted my dilemma and was good enough to assist me.

"I remember what it was like." he laughed.

I've heard many old-timers complain that trucking is not a brotherhood as it once was. I'm sure that is true but, in my own experience, I've found that most drivers are willing to help one another if the situation calls for it. On the other hand, I have encountered the "every man for himself" attitude as well. But the majority of drivers are honest, hardworking men and women who are willing to lend a hand.

After tarping the steel, I was worn out. I was asleep before my head hit the pillow. I would be taking this load to Jacksonville, Florida tomorrow.

Aside from having to wait for over two hours to be unloaded, Jacksonville went well. From there, I went to Georgia Pacific in Savannah to pick up a load of drywall. This one tested my mettle because, not only did I have to back into a tiny dock with my still-limited backing skills, it was also pouring rain, transforming the entire yard into an enormous mud pit. By the time I had secured my load in this veritable pigpen, I probably looked like a creature that had emerged from Scape Ore Swamp in Newberry. As I sloshed back to the cab covered in mud, for a brief instant, I missed my comfortable TV job. I was covered in mud and muck, my feet were wet, and I had sprouted a world-class blister on my right hand. One of the bungee cords had popped off and snapped me in the forehead, so I was wearing an impressive knot as well. As the rain continued to pound down, to my utter astonishment, I began to feel invigorated—even euphoric! I couldn't wrap my mind around it but, for the first time in years, I felt… alive.

I returned to the terminal for a much-needed shower. The muck and grime of the day's labor washed away and along with it, any inclination of returning to my former life. This was still extremely hard on me, but I realized that I was embracing the challenge. Knowing that, the blisters and bumps, along with my weary frame, didn't hurt so much anymore.

My final delivery of the first week went to Alexandria, Alabama. My driver manager tried to give me another run after that, but I told him I was exhausted after my first week and needed to go home. He didn't put up much of a fight and, three hours later, I was back in Scottsboro having completed my first week. The second week, however, would once again cause me to question whether I had made the right decision in becoming a trucker.

Week 2: Accident on I-85

The beginning and the end of the second week truly made me question whether I wanted to be a truck driver. I left on Sunday evening to make a delivery in Greenville, South Carolina. I was driving on I-85 at 10pm, about twenty miles east of Carnesville, Georgia when I felt a jarring **BANG** on the left side of my trailer. My eyes leaped to the mirror to see an automobile hanging in the air at a 45-degree angle before it was swept into a cyclonic whirl. It was a surreal sensation to then watch it flip backward into the nocturnal distance as its headlights blinked away into lifelessness.

The thoughts that enter your mind during a time of shock are often ridiculous. When I lived in upstate New York, I recall going into a skid in my Chevy Nova on an icy winter morning. As my car slid toward a log fence, I remember thinking, just before the moment of impact; *I wonder if my insurance covers this?*

After the car had slammed into my trailer on I-85, I had two thoughts: the first was predictable. *Holy Shit!* The second was: *Maybe no one noticed.* I was so shaken that nowhere on the side of the road looked like a safe place to pull over, so I rolled to the next truck stop. I got out to see the horrific aftermath: bent landing gear a torn mud flap, a dolly crank handle that was twisted into a pretzel, and assorted fiberglass and plastic debris from the car that hit me which was now lodged in the trailer. Yes, someone would notice!

I knew I had to call the authorities, but I first walked into the truck stop in an effort to calm myself to the point where I'd stop shaking. I should have stopped immediately, as soon as the accident happened, but my state of disarray caused me to make the wrong decision. I finally calmed myself and resolved to do the right thing. I went back to the truck and called the police and the company home office. After waiting for over an hour for two officers to arrive, they eventually instructed me to return to the scene of the accident.

When I arrived back at the scene, no one was there. I wondered whether I was in the right place until I saw broken glass alongside the road. I called the police again and finally got in contact with the investigating officer. He told me that the investigation was over, and he didn't need to see me unless I wanted to see him. I politely informed him that I did not. The home office seemed satisfied when I relayed this to them, and I never heard anything more about the matter.

I learned two things from this misadventure: first; safety out here requires being careful <u>and</u> being lucky and, second; I needed to keep my head screwed on straight in a time of crisis. I had made the wrong initial decision, but I had gotten lucky— next time, I might not.

Though there was nothing I could have done to prevent what happened, I hoped that no one was injured. I never found out what caused the accident because the officer didn't tell me, and I didn't want to risk annoying him by asking pesky questions. I returned to the truck stop and removed the two largest pieces of fiberglass from my trailer. I didn't know what kind of car had struck me; the only thing I knew for sure was…it was red.

After delivering to Greenville, I picked up a load in Kinards, South Carolina and took it to Marianna, Florida. The next few days went smoothly and I put the events of Sunday night behind me. Jacksonville is where a fresh, steaming pile of despair waited to squish between my bare rookie toes.

I was to pick up a "drop & hook" load from Celotex, which was adjacent to the Jacksonville terminal. After I *dropped* my empty trailer and then *hooked* up to the pre-loaded one, I intended to shut down for the night at the terminal. But when I moved the truck forward, I heard a sickening, crunching sound that prompted me to stop immediately and look in my mirror. My load leaned and swayed precariously to and fro like a drunken sailor. The look of stunned horror on my face could not have been more profound if I'd suddenly discovered an electric eel clamped onto my crotch.

The "yard dog", or on-site driver for Celotex, had left the dollies up too high when he dropped the trailer. Consequently, when I *thought* I had hooked up to the load, my trailer kingpin had actually traveled past the fifth wheel and snagged onto *something* on the underside of the trailer. But it wasn't actually *hooked* to anything. With more experience, I would have recognized that something was amiss from the "feel", but I was still a rookie who was, apparently, intent on compiling an impressive resume of mistakes. In hindsight, I could have dollied the landing gear to its full height and then used my ratchet bar to manipulate the fifth wheel past the kingpin. But I had not learned this trick yet and I was too upset to formulate a logical solution. I called the home office and they sent a tow truck.

The two hours I spent waiting for the tow truck provided ample opportunity for me to once again question whether I was cut out for this. For all I knew, this would mark the end of my brief trucking career. I had, however, learned another hard and valuable lesson. Thereafter, I visually inspected the lineup of the kingpin to the fifth wheel when I hooked up to a trailer. I still adhere today to this practice…I don't care what other drivers do.

When the tow truck corrected the problem, I took my truck to the terminal shop to ensure that there was no damage to the fifth wheel. The shop technician was a tall, crusty-tempered man named Jack. His face was plastered with the expression of a man who had just found half a cockroach in his breakfast biscuit. He looked to be around 60, and his leathery features appeared to be those of a former boxer who had suffered a broken nose at least a dozen times.

To be sure, Jack was being an asshole of colossal proportions, but instead of countering his verbal diatribe with an attack of my own, I just kept being nice to him. His unpleasantness slowly began to subside, and his disdainful glare was gradually replaced by glances of casual indifference. The fifth wheel was fine, but he found another problem that would require me to leave my truck in the shop overnight. To my utter surprise, Jack called a nearby Econolodge and arranged a motel room for me. He was actually being nice to me now!

After enjoying the comfort of a real bed, I returned to the terminal the next morning to pick up my truck, but it wouldn't be ready until after lunch. My delivery was due in Stockbridge, Georgia this evening but, owing to the delays, I would not make it. I informed dispatch and they told me to drop the load at the Atlanta terminal.

The delay was longer than expected and I didn't get to Atlanta until midnight. I picked up another load at the terminal for a Monday delivery and started heading toward Bridgeport for my "weekend" off. I stopped at a rest area in Resaca, Georgia for a quick respite. When I sat down on the sleeper, my exhausted body convinced me to stay there. I went to bed and rolled into Bridgeport on Saturday morning. This week of hellish misadventure was finally over.

Week 3: School of Hard Knocks

I left on Sunday night to take my load to Greenwood, Mississippi—the site of my very first delivery. Greenwood is known as the Cotton Capital of the world. It also boasts a rich history of the Delta Blues. The legendary Robert Johnson has three memorial gravestones in the Greenwood area and *The King of the Blues*, B.B. King, performed his first live broadcast on Greenwood's WGRM radio station in 1940. Greenwood is also one of the few places in the world where you can stand between two rivers flowing in the opposite direction: the Yazoo River and the Tallahatchie River.[3]

One of the recruiting pitches of some trucking companies is: *Get paid to see America.* In truth, it is extremely rare to get an opportunity to behave like a tourist. You are performing a job and, if you want to make any money, you won't be donning Mickey Mouse ears at Disney World. Even when the occasion presents itself, I typically prefer to relax, watch a movie, and catch up on my sleep. More often than not, truckers are at a loading dock, in an industrial district, at a truck stop, or parked at a rest area or terminal when they shut off the engine…no matter what city they are in.

The delivery in Greenwood went fine this time and, since I had driven the previous night, I went to the Pilot truck stop in Winona, Mississippi to shut down for the evening. I would be picking up at the Georgia Pacific plant in New Augusta, Mississippi in the morning.

When I arrived in New Augusta, the shipping department could not locate my pickup number. This was because dispatch had sent me to the wrong Georgia Pacific plant in the WRONG CITY! They should have sent me to Bay Springs. Drivers and dispatchers often share a forced relationship, and blunders like this do nothing to promote a more harmonious union. By the time I got to Bay Springs, I had probably expended every expletive in the English language, and maybe even the two or three Spanish ones I know.

I picked up a load of lumber in Bay Springs to deliver to Franklin, Tennessee. The trip went nicely and then I was off to Erlanger, Kentucky to pick up a load of ladders. When I got to the weigh station in Simpson County, Kentucky, I was pulled aside for a full DOT inspection. The officer checked everything and, after almost an hour of incessant probing, all he found was a minor defect with one of the trailer air hoses. Fortunately, he did not give me a citation for it and I was on my way again.

When I got to Erlanger, the guard instructed me to drop my empty trailer in a dock and then get my pre-loaded one. My backing skills were slowly improving, but I totally fouled up my effort to get to the loading dock. My rattled nerves caused me to ferry back and forth in a vain struggle for what seemed like an eternity. Another flatbed driver witnessed my strife and came over to offer his assistance. By this time, I was so distraught that I was glad to accept his offer. He made it look easy and, after I thanked him, I made a vow that this would be the last time another driver would have to bail me out of a pickle barrel.

At first sight of the towering mass of ladders I'd be hauling to Frostproof, Florida, I might have been as awe-stricken as the ancient Babylonians peering heavenward at the Tower of Babel. As a rookie, this was the first load of ladders I'd ever encountered and I was having trouble getting past my initial reaction: Damn they were stacked high!

After overcoming my shock and awe, I began throwing my straps across the mountainous heap. I got one of the straps lodged in a pile of ladders and had to climb up and perform a series of contortionist moves to remove it. Then, I missed a throw and the metal end of the strap fell from high above and whacked my forehead, causing me to take a couple of wobbly steps as sparkly little fireflies appeared at the edges of my vision. My knot from Savannah had healed, but this was going to give me a much more impressive one—hell, I was going to have a horn!

I finally secured the load and then I headed back toward Bridgeport. This load was scheduled in Frostproof on Monday, so I left it at the terminal over the weekend. I made it back to Bridgeport and, somehow, I now had three weeks of solo trucking under my belt.

Week 4: Frostproof Ladders and Hooterville

I left for Frostproof on Sunday and this time, I brought Kitty with me. My loyal cat remains my road companion to this day. It took her a little while to acclimate to life on the road but now, she actually gets excited when it's time to go—she knows she gets more treats out here!

Prior to being named Frostproof, the Florida city we were going to was called Keystone City. The name change was a marketing ploy to convince potential landowners that the town would never have a frost that could destroy the citrus-driven economy. About two years after the name change, a terrible frost killed most of the citrus there.[4]

When we arrived, no one was working in the receiving department because today was a holiday. I simply dropped the load in the yard, and the guard signed for it—very easy.

Next, we went for a load of drywall in Apollo Beach that delivered to Atlanta. At this early stage of my trucking career, I still hated going to Atlanta, but this time did not prove to be a problem. A trainer and his trainee, in another company truck, had arrived at the customer before I got there, and they even helped me untarp my load. After delivery, I shut down for the night and picked up the next morning in Opelika, Alabama to deliver to Milton, Florida.

The directions to the customer in Milton would bear out to be another botched offering from the company. My instructions said to go west on US90 when they should have told me to go east. When it became apparent I was going the wrong way, I stopped in front of a motorcycle shop to ask directions from three bikers. They were happy to help, and their instructions were on the money. I turned around at a Walmart and finally found the customer—thanks to the bikers. In general, truckers and bikers have mutual respect born largely from similar challenges in sharing the road with four-wheelers.

After Milton, we set out for Georgia Pacific in Louisville, Alabama. The rural town of Louisville was out in the sticks of Alabama and the narrow, two-lane journey through the boondocks to get there was not my idea of a good time. This load would be going back to Frostproof. I was sure this run would cause me to go beyond my legal hours to work, but dispatch had pressured me into taking it, and I was still too new to put up much of a fight. Experience would teach me that many, if not most, dispatchers will pressure a driver into taking a run that he/she cannot do legally, and then they'll just as quickly rat him out to the safety department for an hours of service violation…after the freight is delivered, of course. A driver must learn to look out for himself or he likely will have a short trucking career.

As I approached Gainesville on Friday morning, after spending the night at a Florida rest area, I noticed a dark SUV deliberately staying beside me on my left. I'm not sure how long it had been there because I was still shaking the morning cobwebs from my head. I slowly peered that way and my mouth went agape as I saw two young women in the vehicle, and the one in the passenger seat had lifted her tee shirt to her neck to expose her breasts. James, from trucking school, would have been drooling like an alley cat at a fish fry.

The only reaction I initially mustered was a stoic look of shock. My personality is typically reserved, but this situation practically demanded a call to action. I flashed a thumbs-up sign and honked the horn in grateful acknowledgment of the presentation. This prompted the driver to pull down the right side of her blouse and offer a bonus exhibition before they zoomed on past. I wasn't sure of the mile marker I was currently at, but I was sure that I had just crossed the city limits of "Hooterville."

As they went past, I spotted a University of Florida sticker on the rear window, so there was a good chance that they were college students. Morning's light was now fully cast. I was awake and alert and, just for today, I was a Gator fan.

In Frostproof, we sat for over two hours because the company had failed to make an appointment for the delivery. When I was unloaded, I went back to Apollo Beach to pick up another load of Gypsum board that the company wanted me to drop in Atlanta. As expected, I had already exceeded my legal allotment of driving hours by the time I arrived, so I had to spend the night at the terminal. I did not get home until noon on Saturday. My "weekends" at this company were getting progressively shorter.

To this point, the company had paid plenty of lip service to the *"We care about our drivers"* theme, but the actions just weren't reflecting the claims. In reality, they cared about the freight being delivered...period. Whether a driver had an acceptable quality of life seemed to be a secondary concern if, in fact, it was a concern at all.

Week 5: Slip Sliding Away

With a few minor exceptions, the fifth week went rather well from start to finish. My first drop was in Evans, Georgia, an affluent suburb of Augusta. Despite having to squeeze in beside another company truck to untarp, the two drivers, another trainer and his trainee, assisted me in my task. To this point, most of the other company drivers I had encountered were genuinely helpful people.

After Evans, we (Kitty and I) picked up lumber at The Timbermen in Camak, Georgia, where I ran into the same two guys again. Camak is a small railroad town that serves as a junction to Savannah, Atlanta, Macon, and Augusta. The railroad, a rock quarry, and the lumberyard serve as the primary industries there. After Camak, we spent the night at the Bridgeport terminal and delivered, the next morning, in McMinnville, Tennessee. Next, we'd be picking up in Cumberland City, Tennessee.

Cumberland City is the site of a huge TVA power plant along the Cumberland River that provides power to much of the area. The plant's massive towers are visible from up to 30 miles away, but I'd be surprised if the belching white smoke that coughs out of the towers has ever appeared on a postcard. While the rolling hills and open space in this area are quite lovely, the unsightly smoke that spews forth from the colossal towers is akin to adorning Miss America with a potato sack.

Cumberland City would become one of my least favorite places to go for many reasons, not the least of which was the small docks at the shipper. They were difficult for me with my ungainly backing skills. Today, I had the added obstacle of a slippery sheet of ice in front of my dock. I felt like throwing my ratchet bar at one of the yard dogs as he pointed and laughed as I sat there spinning—some people just have no class. After about fifteen minutes of anguish, I finally slipped and slithered my way into the dock.

This was only the beginning of the fun. Since it had rained the previous night and then dropped below freezing temperature, my rolled-up tarp was frozen solid. I had to pound on it with a mini sledge for another fifteen minutes to get it unrolled. By the time I had secured my load, all sensation in my hands and feet were gone.

We delivered to Marietta, Georgia the next morning and, after enduring a considerable traffic backup on the Atlanta bypass, we made it to Cottonton, Alabama in time to pick up another load that evening. Afterward, I shut down for the night and I actually made it home early on Friday morning. Overall, this had been a blissfully uneventful week. Maybe I was starting to get the hang of this.

Week 6: French Lick and the Forest

We set out for Vincennes, Indiana at 2am on Monday. Vincennes was originally established in 1732 as a French fur trading post and it stands as the oldest town in Indiana.[5] It is also the birthplace of the legendary Clown Prince of Comedy, Red Skelton.

I made a wrong turn on the way to Vincennes and this cost me about half an hour. I was kicking myself for following the route suggestion of the company instead of a course that made sense. The company sometimes calculates routes "as the crow flies" or, to avoid toll roads. I eventually learned to use a combination of the company's advice, the directions suggested by my own software, and good old common horse sense to decide on a plausible itinerary.

At any rate, we made it to Vincennes and the delivery went fine. A female forklift driver became enamored with Kitty as the cat crawled into my lap and peered curiously out the window. Kitty was overcoming her misgivings about being on the road, and she was becoming increasingly inquisitive about her ever-changing surroundings.

From there, we went to the Gypsum plant in Shoals, Indiana. We were delayed by a painfully long funeral procession on the way and, although I did not wish to be disrespectful, I could not help but to telepathically hurry them along…I was pretty sure the guy in the back of the hearse wouldn't mind.

The Gypsum plant in Shoals was an unexpected respite, because there was a crew of workers who tarped and strapped the load for me—unlike Cumberland City, where they do absolutely nothing. By the time I was loaded, my legal working hours were almost expired, so we shut down for the night on the side of the road in Hoosier National Forest. As the sun set behind the 200,000 acres of thick, deep woods, we were covered by a blanket of darkness that was so absolute, I couldn't help feeling a little spooked.

The next morning, the narrow and winding US150 to Louisville, Kentucky seemed as if it would never end. I shuddered at the prospect of breaking down at 3am in a place called French Lick.

This delivery was going to my hometown—Huntsville, Alabama. I received a warm "Welcome home" greeting upon arrival when the driver of a pickup truck gave me the finger as I was turning into the customer's parking lot. Apparently, he felt that either I had cut him off or that his destination was much more crucial than mine. During my time on the road, I have received the "One-fingered Salute" many times, but I have gotten to the point where my reflex response is, purely, to wave back cheerfully. Another driver told me that he smacked his lips profusely to offer a loving kiss to the "finger man" upon being paid this gesture.

The rain was pouring down in buckets as I got out to untarp my load. I had bought a rain slicker with a hood, but I had yet to invest in a good pair of waterproof boots. My shoes and socks were soaked by the time I was done, and my mood had become as foul as the weather. It got no better when I discovered that we'd be going back to Cumberland City to pick up our next load.

Cumberland City, however, went well this time and, as before, we delivered to Marietta, Georgia. My cooling system was running a little hot, so I informed my driver manager and he brought me back to Bridgeport to have it checked. After learning that I wouldn't get my truck back until sometime the next day, I decided that I'd had enough for this week. I announced to my driver manager that I was going home for the weekend. This earned me a dirty look from him but, apparently, he wasn't in the mood to be confrontational beyond that.

It was now mid-January. Since I was running southeast regional, I had yet to be introduced to the challenges offered by a northern winter. I would later drive nationally for another company, and it was here that I would identify my least favorite aspect of trucking—dealing with inclement winter weather.

Detour: Trucking in a Winter Blunderland

Our first digression from the story explores some of the later misadventures in winter weather. Winters in the southeast can, occasionally, get nasty but, during my first year on the road, I never encountered conditions that presented much adversity. I was in for a rude awakening when I then began driving nationally for a new company. I had experienced harsh winters in Connecticut, when I was in the Navy, and during the three years I lived in upstate New York. But neither of them prepared me for the icy blasts of Minnesota or the bone-chilling winds howling off Lake Michigan, which seemed to freeze the very marrow in my bones.

The tales of my winter woes are many, but I will begin with one that has never left the forefront of my mind:

Shortly after a delivery to Tulsa, I was required to take my truck to a shop in York Haven, Pennsylvania for repairs. When it was determined that I would be there for three to four days, my terminal manager instructed me to move into a new truck which was there on the premises. I'll refrain from using my terminal manager's real name, so I'll just call him "Dick."

Dick, apparently, was under the impression that moving into another truck is as simple as throwing a bag over your shoulder and picking up the new keys. He requested that I move into the new truck and then, take another load that day. To condense a lively exchange into one word—I told him "no."

The process of moving into a different truck, when your supplies are outfitted to stay on the road between three and six is, at least, a two to three-hour endeavor. On this day, when there was a foot of snow on the ground and it was still falling steadily, it took about four hours to complete the transition. By the time I was finished, I was worn out, my feet were wet, and even Kitty meowed in irritable yowls. I wasn't about to take another load today!

We slept in the new truck in the shop yard that night under an increasing blanket of snow. It snowed all night, and when I woke up the next morning, the truck was practically buried—the snow was all the way up to the doors. The shop personnel eventually came out and plowed the parking lot and, shortly thereafter, I accepted a load to Iowa. About the time I had completed my trip plan, my phone rang—it was Dick.

Apparently, "we" had made a mistake by moving into this truck. This one was assigned to another driver. Dick kept using the personal pronoun "we" in reference to the error. I was tempted to ask him if he had a mouse in his pocket. I was going to have to take this truck to our terminal in New Kingstown, PA and then, move into another one! I was not happy!

When I finished cursing Dick under my breath, I set out on an arduous journey to New Kingstown. The road conditions were awful! Cars and trucks were scattered along the shoulder and the median as if they'd been involved in a demolition derby. It soon became apparent that leaving the yard in York Haven had been a huge mistake. Shortly after this epiphany, I got stuck on an off-ramp.

I called the company's number for breakdown services and they could not offer an estimate of how long I'd have to wait for assistance—they were being bombarded with calls from drivers in distress today. Fortunately, a local police officer stopped to check on me, and he had a tow truck on the scene in just a few minutes.

Under normal circumstances, the terminal in New Kingstown is somewhat of an eyesore, but nothing had ever looked as beautiful when I finally rolled into its icy lot. When I found my "new" truck, my heart sank. It was an old ramshackle piece-of-crap from the Mesozoic era. I shook my head and decided that I wasn't going to do another thing today—I was going to take a 34-hour restart here.

I slipped and slid my belongings into the "new" truck the next morning. It was a Freightliner, but in honor of Eddie Albert's tractor on *Green Acres*, I called it my Hoyt Clagwell. When I moved Kitty into her new home, her first reaction was to hiss at the Hoyt Clagwell—it would prove to be an appropriate response.

At long last, we settled into the Clagwell and got our first load assignment to Grandview, Washington. On top of everything else, one of my molars was beginning to abscess, and a cocktail of aspirin and Ora-Jel only served to dull the pain a fraction. Things couldn't possibly get any worse—could they?

We would be picking up our Grandview load from a shipper in Milton, PA. On the way to Milton, I had to make a sudden stop when a traffic backup appeared around the bend. Upon doing so, a three-inch chunk of ice slid off the top of the trailer and snapped my air hoses in two. I managed to pull alongside the road as the low-level air alarm bellowed its mournful timbre, and the sickening hiss of escaping air pressure filled my ears, and drained my resolve. We were stuck on the side of the road in the middle of nowhere.

Fortunately, it took only an hour for a road maintenance truck to arrive and replace my hoses. However, after going about a mile down the road, I saw that there was still a slow leak. I could not believe my run of luck, but I decided to go ahead and pick up my load before I took my truck to the Petro in Milton to have them fitted correctly. This, luckily, did not prove to be a poor decision. The trio of Kitty, the Clagwell, and me would make it to Washington without further incident but, after that, fate would flush a cherry bomb down our crapper once again.

After delivering in Grandview, we set out for Sumner, Washington to pick up our next load. The weather had been beautiful for the past two days, but this all changed on the way to Sumner. As we approached Snoqualmie Mountain, near Hyak, Washington on I-90, I saw the dreaded flashing sign that I hoped I'd never see: *Chains Required.*

Being a Southern boy, I had never put on a set of chains in my life, even though I'd lived in New York for three years. My trainer had given me a verbal explanation of the procedure, but he might as well have been explaining the laws of thermodynamics—I didn't have a clue as to how to chain up. As I paced in the snow, vainly searching for a Rosetta stone to guide me, a driver named Mike, who was pulling doubles, parked ahead of me and began to chain up. I approached him and asked if I could watch, explaining that I had never done it before. I knew that I had about the same chance of successfully putting on a set of chains as I had of building an Egyptian pyramid.

Not only did Mike allow me to watch, he came back and assisted me in putting on my first chain to make sure I got it right. I thanked him sincerely and assured him that I could get the rest on by myself now. It didn't seem so hard now that I had watched someone who actually knew what he was doing. I managed to get the other two on and I felt better, even though I'd lost most of the sensation in my fingers and toes. We made it to Sumner to get our load and, happily, we did not have to put the chains on again when we went over the same mountain in the opposite direction. Our winter adventures, however, were not quite over yet.

While going through South Dakota, the icy road conditions were comparable to what they had been in Pennsylvania on the day I'd gotten stuck on the off-ramp. Four-wheelers littered the shoulder and median of the interstate, and I saw no less than five jack-knifed big trucks keeping them company. A four-wheeler crawled through the icy slush at such an indescribably slow pace that I knew I'd either have to try and go around him or park alongside the road for a few minutes. I opted to pass. I moved into the left lane and began my advancement. The two vehicles were side-by-side as we approached a curve. In the crux of the curve, as I clung to the steering wheel with a white-knuckled "Kung-fu" grip, Kitty decided this was the perfect time to jump into my lap!

I shouted in surprise but, unfortunately, the noise also startled Kitty, who then sunk her claws deeply into the flesh of my thigh. With extreme difficulty, I harnessed my natural instinct to stand up and yell an expletive. I then got to the task of gently prying

Kitty's claws from my flesh while I navigated the icy curve with a fidgety four-wheeler beside me. Happily, we came out of this situation unscathed but, despite the reading of seven degrees on my outside thermometer, I realized that I had broken into a sweat.

Both Kitty and I have also had some winter adventures that, in retrospect, seem comical. I once let Kitty out at a rest area in Montana to play in the snow. The sun had been out the day before, causing some of the ice to melt before the temperature dropped back below freezing. This resulted in a thin sheet of ice covering the snow. After her initial intrigue, Kitty decided that she didn't like the ice that crackled beneath her paws and caused her to sink. She was, in fact, meowing in angst, and I couldn't help being a bit amused by her plight as I retrieved my camera to memorialize this event. By the time I'd snapped a couple of photos, her panic had escalated past funny, and I rescued the frightened feline from her icy mire. As I held her in my arms, Kitty shot a searing gaze at me that conspicuously appeared to be a "screw you" look. I guess I couldn't blame her.

The occasion on which I was, literally, the butt of the joke happened in Ohio. It was snowing heavily when we arrived at our shipper, and when I asked the Shipping Clerk where he wanted me to put my empty trailer, he vaguely replied, "Down at the end." Well, there was nowhere to put it "down at the end" so, I turned to circumnavigate the building in an attempt to find the "end" to which he might be referring. It didn't take long to see that this had been a mistake—there were snow and ice everywhere! I, sadly, recognized this too late, and I was doomed to be stuck while attempting to back out. After a series of failed efforts to dislodge the truck from its bog, I had no choice but to call for a tow truck.

While waiting for help to arrive, I could no longer ignore the need to heed nature's call, so I went into a wooded area to attend to business. The woods were not very dense, and there were railroad tracks very close to my chosen spot. It should not have surprised me to hear the rumble of a train as soon as my pants were around my ankles.

I pondered the irony when I recalled that, not so long ago, I had complained to my landlord about the broken blinds in the bathroom of my upstate New York apartment. Now, I was perfectly comfortable in flashing a vertical smile to a passing train while squatting like a Bluetick hound.

My metamorphosis into a trucker was complete.

Week 7: Bear Creek, Egypt, and Kitty

We began this week early as we left on Sunday morning to return to Jackson, Tennessee; the home of the world's most famous railroad engineer, Casey Jones. We would be picking up another load of steel to deliver to Baldwin, Florida, a small town about 19 miles west of Jacksonville.

The delivery to Baldwin would have gone splendidly if anyone had told me that I was supposed to back out of the unloading area to exit the plant. I drove straight through, expecting there to be an exit in the back of the facility—there wasn't! I had to perform a series of *Cirque du Soleil* maneuvers to get back to where I had entered. Many customers and shippers post signs to direct the driver or, the guard will provide verbal instructions. Others could not care less. I was in a foul mood when I arrived at the Jacksonville terminal to spend the night.

On Tuesday morning, we went to Savannah to pick up a load at Gold Bond, and we ran into Ringo for the first time since I'd gone solo. He had a new trainee in tow, and we would both be delivering to Bear Creek, Alabama the next morning. It hurt my pride a little when he chided me for taking so long to get to Baldwin so, I was inwardly amused when I beat him to Bear Creek by almost an hour.

Bear Creek's claim to fame is that their Phillips High School football stadium was the first in the state to be lighted.[6] To an outsider, this might seem trivial, but in Alabama, where football is a religion, anything pertaining to the pigskin is a big deal. After Bear Creek, Ringo and I met again at the Bridgeport terminal, but our ways then parted as his next delivery was to Jacksonville and mine was to Saltillo, Mississippi.

The delivery in Saltillo went fine except for a daunting steep hill followed by a subsequent drop-off to get into the receiving area at the customer. Aside from being a little scary, it was a painless delivery. Then we were off to Macon, Mississippi to pick up a load of lumber going to Millwood, Kentucky.

On the way out of Macon, I passed through a Mississippi community called Egypt. I immediately burst out laughing with the knowledge that I had now, officially, arrived in Bumfuck, Egypt.

The remainder of the week was without incident, and we got back to Bridgeport late on Friday evening. Upon arriving home, Kitty had come to expect her weekend reward—a jar of baby food. I had begun a tradition, which still continues, of treating Kitty to a jar of Gerber as a homecoming bonus. I realized that I was attaching anthropomorphic characteristics to an animal, but it was difficult to do otherwise when I spent far more time with my cat than with any other human. Besides, she often displayed human-like characteristics.

For example, I once made the mistake of buying a cheaper brand of baby food for Kitty's reward. She sniffed it, turned her nose up, and met my eyes with a disgusted glare. She may be only a cat, but it was apparent that she was capable of discerning quality. From that point on, I purchased only Gerber.

Aside from having to fight with my driver manager again to get home, this week had gone pretty well. The next week, however, would provide me with the most frightening moments that I have experienced since I've been a truck driver.

Week 8: Mountain Man

The first delivery of a new week returned me to Huntsville, Alabama. Although I lived in Huntsville for almost twenty years after I got out of the Navy, it was only recently that I finally visited the facility that Huntsville is most famous for—the Space and Rocket Center. Huntsville's Space and Rocket Center is home to the world-famous Space Camp. I recall, as a little boy, being mesmerized by watching the sky over Huntsville transform into an array of kaleidoscope colors as engineers tested rocket fuels. This dazzling display set the wheels of imagination and dreaming into motion in a young boy's mind.

As a middle-aged man, I still harbor hopes and dreams with the firm belief that we are never too old to pursue them. As age progresses, many tend to write off dreams as silly or inconsequential because the odds are stacked against us. However, if dreams had favorable odds, they would probably be called "likelihoods" or "favorable chances." I, for one, don't think that I have ever felt a magical surge of hope and anticipation that compares to the thrill of reaching for the stars. I believe that life's richest moments are attained by reaching for an unlikely goal. The journey, in fact, may prove just as enlightening as the reward of reaching the destination. While it is true that we cannot make a crater every time we shoot for the moon, that doesn't mean that we should stop trying…perhaps it's just a sign to adjust our aim a little. With that, I'll close the chapter on my road-apple philosophy for today.

Leo, the forklift driver in Huntsville, had a terrible cold today. He said that it was probably from working in the chilling rain from when I'd been there two weeks prior. I can still feel my soaked gloves and socks from that day—Yuck!

After Huntsville, we were off to deliver to Stallings, North Carolina and then, we went to pick up in Prosperity, South Carolina.

Prosperity formerly went under the name, Frog Level. The most popular legend of how the name originated tells of a pond infested with innumerable frogs. A local man is said to have become intoxicated and fell asleep while lying at the end of the pond. When he awoke, the frogs were croaking and he, still being in a drunken stupor, imagined that they were crying, "Frog level."[7] The old name must still hold a bit of influence because Prosperity now holds an annual "Hoppin' Festival" in which a *Hoppin' Pageant Queen* is elected.

Regardless of the distinct honor that it would have been to meet the reigning Hoppin' Queen, I had to pick up my load to deliver to Vonore, Tennessee. This is where things got interesting.

On the way to Vonore, I missed the road I meant to take and, from looking at my map on the fly, I devised a "Plan B" that would prove worthy of its own wing in the *Bonehead Hall of Fame*. I ascertained that I could follow US431 through Pigeon Forge and Gatlinburg and then, cut across on Highway 73 to get back to my road. If I had taken the time to study my map closely, I would have seen the folly of this decision. What I did not know, at the time, was that the path I had chosen would take me directly toward Clingman's Dome, the highest point in Tennessee!

Suffice it to say that this Smokey Mountain trail was not designed with eighteen-wheelers in mind. The truck laboriously crept up the mountain in second gear as the hairpin curves made my stomach churn. It was now obvious that this had been a mistake of epic proportions, but there was absolutely nowhere to turn around; the only thing I could do was keep crawling skyward. Kitty also sensed the tension of our predicament and hid beneath the seat. I would have liked nothing better than to crawl under there with her, but I knew I had to get us out of this mess somehow.

I finally came upon a small guard shack, but the mountain appeared to continue its ascent beyond the shack. My heart sank to my shoe soles when the guard told me that the road dead-ended at the top, and there would be nowhere to turn around. What the hell was I going to do?

Fighting off the urge to start blubbering like a little girl, I began to study my immediate surroundings. A small grassy area behind the guard shack was flanked by a double row of ditches. Flared metal poles inserted into the ground at uneven intervals peeked perilously above the grass like leaden cobras. Under normal circumstances, I would never have considered taking a truck into a precarious space like this, but it appeared to be my one-and-only option.

I said a little prayer and the guard wished me good luck. To make matters worse, the automatic transmission on the Mack was beginning to overheat, and it was increasingly difficult to get it to lock into gear. I would be glad that my next truck would not have an automatic transmission. As I warily entered the grassy area, I knew there was no room for error. The deep ditches on both sides of me promised a severe penalty for blunder. If my trailer went too far into one of them, at best; I would be stuck, at worst; the truck could roll over! I don't think I had trembled and sweated this much since I'd gotten my first real kiss from a girl when I was fourteen.

I destroyed the metal pole sticking out of the ground to my left as I rigidly maneuvered the truck between the two ditches. The guard, who was watching with nervous anticipation yelled, "Don't worry about it man! Just do what you have to do!"

By the time I had negotiated the narrow course and brought the truck safely back to the mountain trail, I had made innumerable vows to start attending church and to never again forget Mother's Day, the birthday or anniversary of any of my friends, Veteran's Day, Memorial Day, Groundhog Day, or even National Kazoo Day. Despite knocking over most of the guard's cones, he ran up to my window and let out a hearty "WOO-HOO!"

"Damn!" he panted, "I never thought you were going to make it!"

"Neither did I," I conceded as I mopped the perspiration from my forehead with an equally sweaty arm.

I attempted to get out and help him set his cones upright, but he waved me off. He was probably just as glad to get rid of me as I was to get out of there. I decided that I would never do another "on the fly" route change in an unfamiliar area again.

I arrived in Vonore about an hour late for my appointment and had to sit for an additional two hours to be unloaded. The customer in Vonore had a "Row of Shame" to which tardy drivers were directed to go sit and wait. I didn't even care. I was just happy to have emerged intact from the mountain fiasco. After Vonore, we delivered to Simpsonville, South Carolina and then, we went back to Camak, Georgia to pick up more lumber. In Camak, I would meet another driver who possessed all the charm of a bull shark with hemorrhoids.

The flatbed driver who was behind me in the loading line, apparently, took offense when I didn't move to allow him into my spot before I secured my straps. I had waited for the guy ahead of me to get his straps on, so I didn't see any reason why I should move before I had mine on. But *Mr. Sunshine* did not share the same sentiment because he pulled ahead of me in the cargo area in an attempt to block me in. He was as pissed off as a hornet with a blunted stinger, and I was getting pretty cranky as well. Nonetheless, I had no desire to go to jail today for planting my ratchet bar across his teeth so, I got back into my truck and eked past him despite his best effort to prevent my progress. I'll admit that it gave me infinite delight as I watched his eyes widen in horror as my trailer edged past his tractor with a dime's-width clearance. I offered him the bonus of a one-fingered salute as I left the yard with a devious smile of satisfaction plastered to my face.

This load was scheduled for delivery in Bartow, Florida. I knew that this would run me over hours and eliminate my weekend so; I called my driver manager and told him I would drop it in Savannah. I didn't ask him if I could—I told him that I would! I was rapidly losing the wide-eyed gape of a rookie, and I was getting fed up with the end-of-the-week antics of the company. My driver manager argued, but he finally relented.

I dropped my load in Savannah and picked up another one to take back to Bridgeport. Even so, it was after midnight on Saturday morning before I got back. This crap was getting old! It's not what I'd signed on for, and it's not what I'd been promised. I was already beginning to question my future with this company.

Week 9: Trucking, Fort Rucker, and Einstein

The most beautiful thing we can experience is the mysterious. It is the source of all true art and all science. He to whom this emotion is a stranger; who can no longer pause to wonder and stand rapt in awe, is as good as dead: his eyes are closed.
-Albert Einstein

The beginning of the ninth week of my trucking career sent me to Swansea, South Carolina. Jesse James is said to have attended a church service at Sharon Crossroads Methodist Church near Swansea. Witnesses have attested that Jesse wore his sidearm in church and sat with his back to the wall during the service, fearing some type of ambush.[8]

Like Jesse, I also felt backed into a corner when I got a first look at the freight I'd be picking up. It was a massive array of steel girders, piled to the sky. The beams, being of different lengths and widths, made it appear that this "top-heavy" load might suffer some stability issues. To alleviate my concerns, I secured it using every single strap that I had on board. We spent the night at an abandoned store in Ulmer, South Carolina and then set out at 1am the next morning. This load was headed to a military base at Fort Rucker, Alabama.

Fort Rucker is the primary flight training base for Army Aviation and is home to the U.S. Army Aviation Warfighting Center and the U.S. Army Aviation Museum. Fort Rucker is often referred to as "Mother Rucker." This serves as both an insulting pseudo-homonym and defers to the birth of an Army Aviator's career and his or her constant return to the post for continued training. It is common knowledge in an Army Aviation career that "Everyone returns to Mother Rucker." [9] My first visit here would, indeed, prove to be a "Mother Rucker" for me!

Upon arrival, the gate guard instructed me to "Keep straight and you can't miss it." There were two things wrong with these instructions: First, I didn't know what the heck "it" was. I assumed the steel would be going to a hangar, but there were hangars all over the place! Second, he should have said, "Veer right," because when I "kept straight," I dead-ended into a road with no place to turn around.

I sat directly across from the Flight School building and, since I had no idea where to go, I got out and walked toward the school to ask someone for directions. Before I got to the door, a white pickup truck stopped alongside me and spat out a hyperactive little old man, who looked to be at least 70. He raced toward me with flailing arms as expletives spewed from his mouth like a geyser.

"I've got to talk to that fucking guard!" he exclaimed. "You're the second truck this morning to come down here, and there's no place for you to turn this son-of-a-bitch around."

Tell me something I don't know, I thought.

He was the project manager for the new hangar that was under construction, and I couldn't prevent being amused by his Einsteinian hairstyle. His twig-like frame and agitated manner added the finishing touches to a comical portrait. However, I was not pleased with taking another dive into the all-too-familiar "pickle-barrel" once again.

"How are you at backing?" he shouted.

"Well," I said, "I'm not the best, but I always get the job done."

His ears, apparently, shut down after he'd heard "I'm not the best..." because from that point on, he began shouting instructions at me on how to drive my truck. He launched the commands in zealous blasts, and my initial amusement with this hyperactive Einstein look-alike quickly altered into a desire to plant an E=MC square-toed boot up his backside! To this point, however, I had humored him and held my tongue.

Finally, when I could endure no more of his verbal assaults, I asked him to get off of my truck with forced politeness. "I'll get it where it needs to go," I assured him through clenched teeth.

"You'll never get it through that gate with your trailer way over there," he submitted. "You weren't listening to me!"

"I appreciate your *help*," I answered sarcastically with a reddening face, "but I think I can get it in there if you step out of the way."

"Well, I hope so!" he puffed as he raised his hands in disgust.

It was a very tight turn but, when my trailer cleared the gate by a full three inches, I could not subdue a satisfied grin. Little Einstein's hyperactivity wound down to a sour frown. He now bore the distinct look of a man who had just bitten into an oil rag.

Eventually, the old guy reassembled the broken pieces of his megalomania and climbed up to my window.

"Well, you got some experience today!" he shouted.

"Yeah," I said. *And not just in truck driving*, I thought to myself. After that, I didn't see the skinny little SOB again.

It took over four hours to be unloaded because the steel had been fashioned in such a haphazard manner that it had to be taken off one piece at a time. One of the workers broke three of his fingers during the ordeal. I called my driver manager to let him know of the delay and told him that I might have to quit if I were ever sent back to Fort Rucker. He laughed as if I was joking—I'm not sure I was.

After the debacle at Fort Rucker, I was glad to be getting out of there. Good riddance! We would be going back to Cottonton, Alabama to pick up more lumber. I would be out of hours by the time I got there, but I knew there was ample parking space to shut down for the night there.

When we arrived, I took a brief jaunt into the woods and, as I returned, I stopped abruptly at the sight of my truck silhouetted against a beautiful sunset. Cascading hues of orange and red spilled from the sky and splashed down to bathe the truck in a stunning aura. I stood frozen at the magnitude and sheer beauty of this moment and, for an instant, I was perfectly at peace with my new job and with the decisions I had made. For the first time since I'd been doing this, I felt a wave of serenity wash over me as if God were telling me, "It'll be okay."

Today had offered my first look at the range of wild emotions provided by life on the road: from blood pressure-raising stress and aggravation to, literally, feeling at one with the universe. If one has the stomach to endure the ride, it is often difficult not to jump in line for a second turn.

Week 10: Loafers and Burmese Chickens

Kitty and I set out for Ocala, Florida on Sunday, and spent the night at the Florida Welcome Center on I-75. This would be the first time that I'd been back to Ocala since my family vacationed there when I was a young boy. We had visited Silver Springs, just east of Ocala. Silver Springs is a 350-acre nature theme park that surrounds the headwaters of the Silver River, the largest artesian spring formation in the world. [10]

After exploring the park and taking the glass-bottom boat ride in the summer of 1970, my father, mother, sister and myself, returned to our motel room in Ocala. Our family pet was a grouchy toy poodle named, ironically, Ringo. My father put Ringo on a leash, and the whole family went out for an evening stroll. Dad had purchased a new pair of dark brown, suede loafers specifically for this trip. He had bragged all day about how he felt as if he were "walking on air."

"These are the most comfortable shoes I've ever worn," he boasted.

My dad was in love with his new loafers.

As we walked, Dad stopped along the way to chat with some other tourists. As he talked, Ringo incessantly tugged on his leash as if he harbored a sense of urgency about something. My father was so engaged in his conversation that he seemed oblivious to the imploring yanks of the little dog—he just automatically reeled the animal back in. Even at eight years old, it was obvious to me that the tiny poodle required…something. Then, without pomp or fanfare, we all discovered what that *something* was.

Ringo politely lifted his hind leg and urinated all over my dad's dark brown, suede loafers. At first, everyone stood stunned and mute, while my father wore the shocked expression of a man who had just been told by his doctor that he has 24 hours to live. My mother was the first to emit a snicker. This provided the permission I needed to release the enormous guffaw, which would have caused me to explode had I held it in any longer. Soon, everyone was laughing...except my dad. He tossed the leash of the offending critter to my mother and stormed back to the motel room wearing a sour frown, a set of bulging veins in his temples, and a precious pair of dark brown, suede loafers that were soaked in poodle piss. I was too young to understand it at the time, but I later viewed this incident as a lesson that the most precious belongings in life remain immune to the fate of my father's beloved loafers. In contrast, any of our material belongings runs the risk of being piddled upon without warning. To this day, the "loafer incident" remains a legendary source of amusement for me and my family.

The delivery to Ocala went fine, but the traffic was ridiculous in this tourist town. I was glad to get out of there and head toward Palatka, Florida to pick up a load of Gypsum board to take to Stallings, North Carolina. Kitty now enjoyed peering out the floor window on the passenger door as we rode along. She seemed to like being on the road now.

From Stallings, I was slated to pick up a load of steel in Columbia, South Carolina to deliver to the Mayo Clinic in Jacksonville. The only problem was that dispatch didn't send me any directions or a valid contact number for the Jacksonville destination. I called my driver manager to request the information I needed.

"Sure man!" he eagerly replied.

Two hours later, I still had nothing. So, I called Ringo (the person) on his cell and asked his advice. He gave me a suggestion that I took.

I called my driver manager back and told him I would go ahead and take the load, but if I didn't have any information by the time I got there, I'd drop it at the Savannah terminal and let them figure it out. He hesitated a moment and reluctantly said, "Okay." Ten minutes later, I had both my directions and contact number. Thanks, Ringo! After Jacksonville, we went to Fitzgerald, Georgia to pick up lumber.

On the way to Fitzgerald, I went right past the shipper because the log truck ahead of me blocked my view of the sign. I saw it only as I was zooming past. Herein was contained a valuable lesson about big trucks on rural roads: If you miss your turn, there may not be anywhere to turn around for miles. I had to go almost 20 miles before I found a place to turn around.

Fitzgerald, Georgia is a unique town because it is the only city, of which I am aware, where chickens can be seen running around in the downtown area. Not just any chickens, mind you, but wild Burmese chickens. Fitzgerald and surrounding Ben Hill County boasts Georgia's only known wild Burmese chicken population.

In the 1960's, Burmese chickens were stocked all over the state to be hunted like other game birds. For some reason, the chickens never took hold in other areas of Georgia, but they prospered in the downtown area of Fitzgerald.[11] The residents of Fitzgerald have a love/hate relationship with the wild birds. Some folks buy seed and feed them; others chase them out of their yards with a broomstick and a few expletives. But, love 'em or hate 'em, Burmese chickens are a familiar part of the Fitzgerald scene. Fitzgerald may, in fact, be the only city in America where chickens have the right of way.[12]

We delivered our Fitzgerald load to Millwood, Kentucky on Friday, and then went back to Shoals, Indiana for another load. This guaranteed that I would not get home until Saturday. My patience with this trucking company was rapidly wearing thin. I had not, yet, adapted to the lifestyle of an over-the-road trucker.

Week 11: Buckets of Mud

The load we picked up in Shoals was slated for delivery to Huntsville on Monday. Unfortunately, my truck needed repairs, and the delivery had to be rescheduled for Tuesday. When repairs were complete, we delivered to Huntsville and returned to Bridgeport to pick up a load of drywall to take to Hattiesburg, Mississippi. Upon arrival to Bridgeport, the freight was not ready, and we had to wait almost fifteen hours before we got it. This week was shaping up to be a week of delays, which would translate into a crappy paycheck. In theory, the company offered detention pay for delays such as this, but trying to extract it from my terminal manager was about as fun as manscaping with a home waxing kit.

We got our load at 3am and set out for Hattiesburg. When we arrived at the Sherwin-Williams store to deliver the buckets of joint compound (which Ringo called "Buckets of Mud"), another delay awaited us. The unloading process was painfully slow because the forklift being used looked like a battery-operated toy that should have had *Tonka* inscribed on its side. Also, the forklift driver was obviously a rookie as he appeared more qualified to drive a bumper car. As I settled in for a long wait, I took little comfort in the fact that, this time, it was not me who looked like a monkey screwing a football.

About midway through unloading, the forklift driver had, apparently, failed to seat one of the palates correctly on the forks. As he was taking it back to the warehouse, he hit a bump that caused the palate to break, and all of the buckets of joint compound went tumbling into an enormous mud hole.

As he began a long and arduous task of fishing all the buckets out of the mud, I finally took pity on him and got out to assist. My good deed served as a stark reminder that I still had not purchased any waterproof boots. By the time we were unloaded, I was out of hours, so we spent the night behind the Sherwin Williams store.

It rained for most of the night, and it was still raining the next morning when we left for Meridian, Mississippi to pick up lumber. In keeping with the theme of the week, I had to sit and wait on a stopped train for half an hour before I could get into the shipper.

Mid-South Lumber in Meridian was nothing but a giant mud pit. When I had finished strapping and tarping the lumber, I once again looked like the Lizard Man from Scape Ore Swamp. To make matters worse, this load was designed for a 48-foot trailer, and I had a 45-footer. The wood jutted out over three feet from the back of the trailer. As per DOT regulations, I was required to tie a red flag on it, but I didn't have one. Thankfully, the forklift driver saved my behind by finding an old red tee shirt for me. I thanked him but spared him a muddy handshake.

This load would deliver to Morristown, Tennessee, the home of Davy Crockett. The cult-favorite horror movie, *Evil Dead* was filmed off of Kidwell's Ridge Road in Morristown. Sadly, the cabin featured in the movie has since burned down, but the chimney still stands and continues to attract some of the most fanatical devotees of the film.[13]

We arrived in Morristown before noon on Friday, so I fully expected to get a load assignment that would destroy my weekend again. I almost suffered a cardiac arrest when the Qualcomm beeped and the message read: *Head to Bridgeport.* I would actually get home at a respectable hour this week. However, because of all the delays this week, my paycheck was going to be abysmal.

Nonetheless, I was still in a pretty good mood as I drove back toward Bridgeport. I had no idea that the next week would set the stage for my swan song with this company.

Week 12: A Smoke Tarp, The Broken Yolk, and Jack Daniels

My final week with this company started out with a jolt. On the way to Anderson, South Carolina, I slowed for a traffic backup near the Atlanta bypass and became alarmed as white smoke billowed from beneath the hood and impeded my vision. As it turned out, I had just forgotten to replace the cap on the coolant reservoir after my pre-trip inspection earlier this morning. Some of the coolant had splashed out on the engine to cause the smoke. I was relieved to discover that the problem was a minor one, but a sphincter-tightening scare is never a good way to begin a new day.

After Anderson, we went to Duluth, Georgia to get our next load. Duluth elected Georgia's first female mayor in 1922 that promised to "Clean up Duluth and get rid of demon rum."[14] I could have used a slug of "demon rum" when I saw that I would have to blindside into a small dock to be loaded. This would be my first attempt at blindsiding into a dock, but I actually pulled it off quite nicely. I was actually starting to get better at this.

This would be my first stop-off load. A stop-off is when the delivery goes to multiple locations. In our case, we would be delivering to Charlotte, and Concord, North Carolina. I would come to detest stop-offs. They paid $35 extra but, in general, they were seldom worth the extra trouble.

Nonetheless, the stop-off deliveries went well, and then we were off to Statesville, North Carolina to pick up a load of chain-link fence. This was another first for me. Due to the height of the load and the nature of the freight, a smoke tarp would be required. This would prevent the fence from being stained by exhaust fumes. The only problem was that I had never been issued a smoke tarp.

I called my driver manager and he nonchalantly resolved, "Just use a regular tarp." It quickly became evident that he had never climbed atop a towering mass of unstable chain-link fence, and precariously wrestled with a 130-pound tarp in an effort to fashion it into a smoke tarp. By the time I had survived this perilous ordeal, I had vowed that I would never take another unnecessary risk like this. If the company wanted me to pick up another load that required a smoke tarp, they'd better issue me the proper equipment! I had been with this company for less than five months, but I'd already heard of no less than four drivers who had fallen off their loads and injured themselves. I did not want to be the next statistic…they could kiss me where the sun doesn't shine!

I was out of hours when my task was complete so, I walked toward the Shipping Office to ask if I could stay here overnight. The Shipping Clerk was already walking toward me. He was holding new pair of gloves, which he handed to me and said, "Here, take these. It looks like you wore yours out."

I laughed and said, "I don't think that's all I wore out!"

He was happy to allow me to stay overnight, and Kitty was already snoozing when I crawled next to her in the sleeper. This load would be going to Holiday, Florida.

We set out the next morning before any rooster had a passing thought of a cock-a-doodle-doo, and made it just shy of Gainesville before shutting down for the night. I wondered if I'd get another peep show from a passing SUV similar to the one I'd gotten last time but, sadly, I didn't.

When we arrived in Holiday and I found out that the unloading process would be lengthy, I walked across the street and had breakfast at a little restaurant called The Broken Yolk. It had a nice, homey atmosphere and friendly service, but I ordered a heaping mound of food that was served on a platter suitable for a Nordic Viking. My eating habits had suffered since going on the road but, due to the physical nature of flatbed work, I had not gained any weight. In fact, I may have even dropped a few pounds. I had begun to notice, at truck stops, that there were far fewer overweight flatbedders than non-flatbedders. There was a valid reason for that.

When we had ridded ourselves of the chain-link fence, we were off to Palatka, Florida again to pick up more Gypsum board. As I was pulling into the waiting line at the shipper,

Ringo's unmistakable baritone boomed over the CB, "Get it in there Rick!"

"Man," I replied, "they'll let anybody in here won't they?"

"I guess so!" he shot back with a hearty laugh.

After loading, we went back to the Jacksonville terminal to spend the night. There is no lighting in the terminal yard there, so one almost requires the navigational system of a bat to park after dark. At this point in the week, I was in reasonably good spirits. I still had no idea that this would be my final week with the company.

When we set out for Conway, South Carolina on Friday morning, I gave myself an enormous scare on a U.S. Highway. I was fooling around with my sunglasses and, the next thing I knew, the truck had veered off onto the soft shoulder of the road. I'm not sure how close I came to mowing down some mailboxes, but I couldn't have missed by much. This near-miss put the fear of God into me and, after that, I straightened up and got with the program. This had been a frightening reminder that it only takes a split second of inattention for disaster to strike.

When we got to our customer in Conway, I used my trusty roll of duct tape to repair my tarp. On the way to Holiday, the wind ripped a three-foot gash in the seam. It had not, after all, been designed for use as a smoke tarp.

As it turned out, I had plenty of time to make the repair. I waited for over three hours to be unloaded. It was now 2pm on Friday, and I was four hundred miles from home. Once again, I was looking at another ridiculously short weekend at home. I did not have the hours to drive four hundred additional miles today. So, when dispatch sent me a load assignment that would send me even farther away, something just snapped!

I was dirty, tired, hungry, and furious when I called my terminal manager in Bridgeport.

"We'll pay you seventy-five dollars for a weekend layover," he offered.

I can't recall, specifically, if I told him where he could stick his seventy-five bucks, but I'm sure he got the point.

"If you go home, we'll charge you for the fuel," he threatened.

"If you want to screw me out of my last paycheck," I replied, "go ahead…but this isn't what I signed on for—I'm going home!"

With that, I hung up and set out for Bridgeport.

I had driven for about a hundred miles when my phone rang—it was my terminal manager again.

"There's a load you can pick up in Bowman, South Carolina and bring it to Atlanta before you go home," he said.

"I'm almost two hundred miles east of there," I replied. "I don't have enough hours left to do that and, even if I did, I've already told you what I'm doing."

"You'll be charged for the fuel," he repeated.

"I'll talk to you on Monday," I said and hung up the phone.

I pulled into a truck stop shortly thereafter because I was too tired and too upset to keep going. When I'd had time to cool off, I reflected on the events that had just taken place, and wondered whether I had allowed my fatigue and emotions to produce a knee-jerk reaction. I was torn about what I had done, and about what I was going to do next.

It had not sounded like I was going to be fired—just screwed out of my paycheck. My thoughts were tumbling viciously in my mind, and my world seemed surreal. I had serious reservations about quitting now, but I did not relish the thought of crawling back with my tail between my legs. I wasn't sure of anything right now except that I wanted to go home tomorrow and purchase a bottle of Jack Daniels.

Detour: A View from the Cab

After I gained more experience in trucking and adjusted to the lifestyle, I realized that, as trucking companies go, there are many out there that are far worse than my first company. While I still consider my reasons for leaving to be valid, culture shock played a large role in the decision I made on that day. I had, after all, worked in an entirely different world for the past twenty years.

Trucking is not just a job; it is a lifestyle. For most, the transition to the trucking lifestyle is a difficult one. Once again, this is the reason why the vast majority of CDL school graduates are no longer in the trucking business after three months…or less. They are not prepared for the challenges it presents, or for the days and weeks spent away from home and family.

Ultimately, I never regretted my decision to leave my first company because the next one would be an improvement. I would, however, discover some universal truths about the trucking industry that are not always pretty.

One of the first, and most obvious, is that any company engaged in the trucking business is not going to offer the standard amenities that are taken for granted in most other jobs. For instance, sick leave is non-existent in most trucking jobs. If you don't work, you don't get paid…period.

When I worked a "normal" job, it never posed much of a problem if I needed to take half a day off for a doctor's appointment. In trucking, keeping a medical or dental appointment can often be a roll of the dice. You never know if you are going to be home to keep it. I once lost a crown on one of my front teeth and had to drive around for two weeks looking like I had a mouthful of broken pottery.

A typical job always gave me the comfort of knowing that I would go home at the end of a stressful and harrowing day to sleep in my own bed. In trucking, an OTR solo driver eats alone in his truck or at a truck stop at the end of a long day before retiring to the "comfort" of a small and lonely sleeper berth. Then, he gets up after a few hours rest and does it all over again. I never thought that it would be possible to miss the company of some of my annoying former co-workers, but the loneliness of the road is very real.

Trucking is also one of the most regulated industries in America and continues to grow more restrictive to its drivers as time passes. From anti-idling laws to hours of service regulations and the mandating of electronic logs, the trucking industry becomes more invasive to freedom. From law enforcement officials finding any excuse to issue truck drivers costly tickets to companies invading the privacy of drivers with GPS monitors and, in some cases, even video cameras, the freedom of the road is fast becoming a thing of the past. Apparently, lawmakers believe that piling on more and more regulations and continually increasing restrictions will make the road a safer place. In reality, a troubling side effect of super-regulating the industry is that many veteran drivers are getting out of the business and trucks are being filled with rookies. Soon, they'll be gone too, and someone else will take their place…rinse and repeat with a new wash of disposable greenhorns.

It often seems that lawmakers and trucking companies forget that trucks are occupied by real, live human beings who have families, and who would like to have a life outside of that truck. A fundamental indifference to a driver's quality of life can often be seen in the trucking industry and, sometimes, even basic humanity seems to take a backseat to delivering freight. I have experienced it, firsthand. The story goes like this:

Shortly after I arrived in Odessa, Nebraska, my air-conditioning compressor died and it got well above 90° in the truck. I called the breakdown department to tell them that I needed to drop my load at a nearby terminal so that I could have it repaired. The initial reply that I got was, "The Company doesn't consider air-conditioning to be a valid reason not to complete a run."

This reasoning probably derives from "the company" not being the one who is trying to get adequate rest in a ninety-five degree truck so they can drive six hundred miles the next day. If the roles were reversed, I'll bet the pointer on their validity scale would have a dramatic reversal.

I finally had to insist that I would both drop my load at the terminal and get my A/C fixed, or I would turn in my truck at the terminal. Either way, I was going to take this trailer no farther than the terminal. Presented with these options, the company relented and gave me permission to get my A/C repaired.

It boggles my mind when I consider that most people would be prepared to come to blows over having their pet subjected to extreme heat or cold, but many trucking companies and lawmakers pay no heed to a moral thermometer in regard to subjecting truck drivers to sub-standard conditions. This lends support to my assertion that many in the transportation industry appear only to care about the amount of revenue generated—not the welfare of the driver. Despite their sophist rhetoric to the contrary, the reality lies in their actions.

On this occasion, it was necessary to threaten to quit in order to afford myself a fundamental necessity. However, playing the "I'll quit" card isn't always a smart option. If a driver quits when he is a long way from home, and then expects the company to provide him with transportation, he is in for another wake-up call. As another driver points out:

"They will bend you over and give it to you with no Vaseline every time…guaranteed!"

The smart option for a company driver is to suck it up and wait until he is routed home and all of his belongings are removed from the truck. The vast majority of trucking companies will not pay to have personal effects shipped either. At the very least, the vehicle should be turned in at a company terminal and the driver should have the financial forethought to provide his own transportation for himself <u>and</u> his belongings. Believe me, if you get mad and quit when you're in Moose Turd, Ontario, you'd better have a heavy parka and an excellent pair of snowshoes!

When it comes to large trucking companies, there seems to be no way to get past the impersonal nature of it. One of the reasons is that dispatchers are assigned to zones. As a result, the drivers and the dispatchers never get to know one another on an individual basis. To me, the dispatcher in whatever zone I happen to be in is a faceless "John", and to him, I am merely a truck number. I have encountered a few exceptions to this rule, and I tip my hat to the precious handful that has attempted to insert their own personal touch. But in the end, the grinding cogs of the vast corporate mechanism tend to drown out their tiny voices, and the machine spews out a number.

I have often gotten the distinct impression that many managers and dispatchers actually think that they know what road life is like. Having resided on both sides of the fence, I'll say that they can understand the trucking life by sitting behind a desk in the same way I can understand what it's like to be a cowboy by watching a rodeo. I may get a narrow snapshot of what it's like to be a cowboy, but I still have no inkling of the cowboy life.

While sitting in an air-conditioned office, it is impossible to understand what it's like to make nightly applications of Tiger Balm on your feet to prevent a painful Charley Horse from springing up in your arches and waking you up in the night because you spent the day working a stiff clutch through a crowded metropolitan area; or the necessity to urinate in a milk jug; or being forced to drive six hundred miles with a toothache; or the need to spray an anti-fungal agent in your crotch to prevent jock itch that can result from countless hours bouncing and sweating in the driver's seat. Neither, can they understand the need to spend an entire day of precious home time making preparations and re-supplying to go on the road again.

I'll be the first to admit that my "view from the cab" does not adequately consider the inner workings of a trucking company or the stresses, responsibilities, and headaches contained therein. I also concede that successful management does not always coincide with the desires of employees. Despite my railing, I have a high degree of respect for strong, competent, and ethical business leaders. Like truckers, they do not live in a world where "just anyone" can survive and thrive. My contempt is reserved for those greedy and unethical business leaders who line their own pockets like a squirrel stuffing acorns into its cheeks with no regard to the hardworking people who make their standard of living possible. These are the people who feast off the sweat of truckers while throwing them a pittance of crumbs and expecting them to be grateful for the pathetic and inhumane gesture. My contempt is for lawmakers who have never spent a day in the life of a trucker, yet dictate every waking moment of their professional lives with no practical understanding of what they go through. My contempt is for law enforcement officials and lawyers who view truckers as a source of revenue.

The trucking industry sheds a bright spotlight on the fact that there are often ethical conflicts between making money and doing the right thing. In my estimation, the trucking industry lags behind in affording the amenities for drivers enjoyed by the majority of the American workforce. Trucking, certainly, is an industry in which you have to stand up for yourself, or you'll have footprints all over your face.

On a few occasions, people who are considering a career in trucking have asked me about it. The following is my advice to any prospective new truck driver:

- Trucking is a lifestyle more than it is a job. If you are not prepared to make a MAJOR lifestyle change, save your time and/or money and forget about it.

- Research the companies. Check them out online, talk to experienced drivers and do not be afraid to ask questions. Interview the company. Yes, you heard me right. Prepare a list of questions for a company that you are considering and do not be shy about asking them. Any recruiter worth his salt will be glad to indulge you. If he isn't…run like the wind! Go to a truck stop and **talk to truckers** to get straight answers and to separate the wheat from the chaff. A recruiter isn't going to tell you that the company he is recruiting for has a 130% turnover rate among drivers. If a recruiter's lips are moving, there's a good chance that he's lying. If his lips aren't moving, there's a good chance that he's withholding the truth. However, also be wary of excessive adverse reports of a company from a handful of sources. Disgruntled drivers who were fired or denied employment often give negative reviews about their former employers as a tactic of revenge. Do your homework! Research the companies!

• Your first trucking job will probably not be with a blue chip company. The genuinely good companies only hire experienced drivers and many of them do not use recruiters…they don't need to. All but the most fortunate have to pay their dues before they have a fighting chance to get hired by a decent company that will treat them with respect.

• Even the "good" startup companies are going to treat you like a piece of meat. They care about the freight being delivered…period. Your home time, your quality of life, and your job satisfaction are purely secondary concerns. Be prepared for it.

• If you are thinking of becoming an owner/operator, educate yourself as to what this entails. In short, it requires being both a small business manager **and** a driver. I've seen plenty of new owner/operators who were desperate to sell their truck after six months because, quite simply, they were drowning in a sea of debt and cluelessness. I'd recommend that anyone start out as a company driver to ensure that trucking is actually what he or she wants to do for a living. I cannot stress it enough…educate yourself!

• Having said all this, trucking can still be what you make of it despite its many challenges. Even with the ever-mounting regulations and restrictions, it still affords a freedom and autonomy that most other jobs cannot match. Trucking can still be a rewarding career if you have the right disposition for it, but it doesn't come without significant sacrifices. If you aren't prepared to make those sacrifices, don't waste your time and money.

Right, wrong, or moot, this is my view from the cab.

Week 13: Take this job and...

As I had planned, I had a serious conversation with Mr. Jack Daniels when I got home on Saturday. I was confused and depressed, and I questioned whether I was cut out for a trucking life. At this company, I felt like little more than a mooing piece of cattle. I had already cleaned out my truck when I'd gotten back to Bridgeport, so I think that I had already unconsciously made my decision. Be that as it may, I spent the weekend thinking that, perhaps, I'd just accept getting screwed out of my check and tough it out a while longer. I had only been with this company for about five months, and I didn't know how difficult it would be to find another job.

On Sunday, I decided not to invite Mr. Daniels over again because it felt like he'd hit me in the head with a sledgehammer the previous night. I spent the day pondering my options and nursing my hangover. When I went to bed Sunday evening, I was still unsure what I would do when I went to talk to my terminal manager on Monday.

When the alarm rang on Monday morning, my decision became crystal clear as soon as I got out of bed. There was no question in my mind that I had absolutely no desire to drive this week. My mind was made up.

I went to the terminal and quit. It was not an ugly scene; I even shook hands with my terminal manager as I left, and he said that he would provide me with an excellent reference. I had already learned a hard lesson in regard to burning bridges in my former career. Also, a trucking company can make it difficult to find new employment if they are so inclined. A vindictive terminal manager or dispatcher might put misleading or false information on the driver's DAC report. A DAC report is somewhat like a credit report for truckers. Like a credit report, few drivers ever send in for a copy of it, and the employer does not provide one. It is necessary to jump through some hoops to get a copy of the DAC report but, like a savvy consumer, the savvy trucker will always know what is on his DAC report.

Author's Note: *After numerous complaints, (and lawsuits) obtaining a copy of the DAC report is now easier than ever. The company that manages DAC reports is called HireRight, and one need only visit their website to request a free copy of the report. A physical mailing address and a phone number are also provided on the site. While some abuse may still occur, truckers are no longer the helpless victims of false DAC reports like they once were. Here is where to request a copy of the DAC report:*

http://www.hireright.com/Consumers-Applicants.aspx

I was glad that my parting had been painless and friendly, but now, my future was uncertain again. As I drove back to Scottsboro from Bridgeport, I reflected on the positive aspects of trucking. I actually liked the smell of diesel as I walked into a truck stop after shutting down for the evening. The rumble of the powerful engines served as an odd lullaby. I often enjoyed sitting at the end of a long day and drinking in the aroma of the night, and watching the traffic pass by as it left only time in its wake. It was relaxing and cathartic to watch the nocturnal activity as the cool wind caressed my face. In rare times like those, no matter where I was, I felt as if there was no place else I'd rather be, or nothing else I'd rather be doing. Like a runner's high, this was a type of trucker's high. The manifestation of it is rare but, when it happens, everything just sort of feels right with the world. I realized that I already missed the crazy life that I had left behind only moments ago.

The stark reality of uncertainty interrupted my reminiscence, and the insecurity of being unemployed cast a gloomy shadow over me.

Week 14 and 15: Greener Pastures

After I had quit on Monday, I sat around the house for the rest of the week and gained about ten pounds as I seemed intent on testing the limits of two of the Seven Deadly Sins. My money was running dangerously low, so I knew I'd better get on the fast track to gainful employment.

I went online and put in a single application to multiple companies on a trucking website. Within fifteen minutes of submitting an application, my phone rang. Over the next week, I was bombarded with phone calls and e-mails from no less than two-dozen trucking companies. Despite my limited experience, my fears seemed to be unwarranted. Not only did it appear that getting another job wouldn't be much of a problem, I'd even get to pick and choose. This was showing me that the demand for truck drivers is real. I would soon learn that if a driver gets some quality experience under his belt and, most importantly, keeps a clean record, the ability to find a job is the least of his worries.

Author's Note: This experience occurred in early 2006, well before the economic downturn hit its full stride. Following the decline, the experience described above is unlikely to have been replicated. However, as I write the revisions to the 2nd edition in December of 2014, the demand for truckers seems to be as great as it ever was.

I researched some of the companies that had contacted me and narrowed it down to four. I had intended to stay with flatbed, but the flatbed company that I was most interested in could not give me a specific date on which a trainer would be available. Since I had less than six months experience, they would require me to spend two weeks with a trainer. However, my financial situation was becoming dire, and I didn't have time for the uncertainty of a waiting list. Upon further research, I discovered that the other flatbed company on my short list had a poor reputation among many drivers. Now, two companies remained on my list.

I spoke with representatives from both businesses and ultimately decided on a company based in Lincoln, Nebraska. Because I was switching from flatbed to dry van, my new employer would require me to spend six weeks with a trainer. I wasn't thrilled at the prospect of riding with a stranger for another six weeks, but I was excited to be going back to work. This was a large company, but they had a good reputation in most trucking forums, and even a rival company had conceded that they had a good reputation. I had no illusion that any trucking company would be a walk in the park, but I felt that I had made the right choice…I certainly hoped so.

I encountered a few potholes during the application process, but we finally got everything ironed out and I was scheduled for orientation. On the following Saturday, the company supplied me with a rental car to drive to Lincoln. I had never been to Nebraska, so this would be a new adventure. Unlike the disagreeable carpooling of newbies at my former company, I would have a rental car all to myself, and I would not have to share a motel room with a stranger. So far, I already liked this company better.

I had signed on for a southeast regional Coca-Cola/Minute Maid fleet, but I agreed to run nationally while I was with my trainer. I was about to be on the road again.

Week 16: Orientation, Merlin, and a Plumbing Misfortune

Ringo gave me a ride to the Huntsville airport on Saturday to pick up my rental car. He seemed a little disappointed that I had quit, but he was very supportive. I hired his twelve-year-old son to feed Kitty while I was gone, and Ringo agreed to check in on her on the weekends. I hated to leave the little cat alone, but I couldn't bring her with me, and it would have cost a fortune to board her for an unspecified amount of time. I did not know how long it would be before I got back home. After orientation, I would be immediately going on the road with my trainer.

I thanked Ringo, picked up my rental car, and I was on my way. I stopped for fuel somewhere in Illinois and discovered that my credit card had reached its maximum limit. I'd have to rely on my dwindling cash the rest of the way. I spent the night in an unsightly motel in a small Missouri town about eighty miles east of Kansas City, even though I had been tempted to sleep in the car to save money. Despite my worries, I slept well and headed out early Sunday morning.

I arrived at Day's Inn in Lincoln, where I would stay for the duration of orientation, and was greeted by a friendly desk clerk named Chelsea. Before arriving in Lincoln, I'm certain that I had never seen such an abundant landscape of cornfields. It was evident why Nebraska was nicknamed, *The Cornhusker State*.

After getting settled into my room, I returned the rental car to the airport and, since it was only a mile from the motel, I decided to walk back. The walk would have been enjoyable if it hadn't been so darned windy. Remnants of snow remained splotched about from a storm that had passed through last week. As I observed the aftermath of the storm melting away, I hoped that it would serve as a symbolic representation for what lay ahead.

A shuttle bus arrived at 6:30am on Monday to take all of the new employees to the terminal for physicals. At least twenty people of disparate girth crammed into the small vehicle, and I thought that it might be appropriate to add a little mustard—we were packed in like sardines. A petite, dark-haired girl practically sat in my lap. When we arrived at the Lincoln terminal, it was not what I expected. It looked like the Taj Mahal in comparison to the hideous eyesores that passed for terminals at my former company. The huge three-story building was impeccably clean, and the maze of corridors seemed to, ironically, invite the orientation crowd to become **dis**oriented. The building contained a large cafeteria and even a gym. I was again taken aback by the contrast between this and the small, dusty terminals to which I had grown accustomed.

My first moment of horror came early. I discovered that we would have to take our road test *before* orientation, and *before* going out with our trainer. The Century Class S/T Freightliner had a 10-speed manual transmission, and I had been driving an automatic for the past five months. I had not driven a shifter since riding with Ringo, and I expected the road test would happen <u>after</u> getting some practice with my trainer. I was already sprouting nervous beads of sweat.

The man who administered my road test was an old fellow named Bill who wore a cantankerous veneer like a ski mask. At 79-years-old, he still did a dedicated run from Lincoln to Canada and back every week. Bill's initial hard-boiled personality was deceiving as he revealed his true nature when the road tests began. His biting but agreeable humor immediately set me at ease.

"If you don't wreck it, you pass!" he croaked.

My road test went surprisingly well. The Meritor gear shifter in the Freightliner operated more smoothly than the one in Ringo's truck. I even managed to back into a small hole when we returned to the terminal yard. The first thing I noticed was that the closely positioned dual axles on the dry van trailer caused it to react more quickly than the split axles on the flatbed trailers. This was going to take some getting used to.

I shook Bill's hand and thanked him as his initial façade of crabbiness was stripped away to reveal a radiant smile. I then returned to the terminal to wait, fill out additional paperwork, wait some more…wait even more, and finally, go to the doctor for my physical.

The next two days were comprised of the standard orientation rhetoric—some of it useful, some of it sleep-inducing. The dark-haired girl whom I'd gotten to know (almost too well) on the shuttle ride sat at the table directly behind me throughout orientation, and her habit of constantly crunching ice cubes caused me to spend an inordinate amount of time digging my fingernails into my legs. Regardless of this annoying routine, I got to know her during the breaks, and she turned out to be one of the nicest people I would meet there. Her name was Mona, and once she found out who my trainer would be, we had a lot to talk about.

My new trainer was a family friend to Mona, and to her husband, Calvin. Calvin was also a trainer, and he would be training his wife after orientation. On the final day of orientation, Calvin and my new trainer, Merlin arrived. The four of us piled into Calvin's bobtail truck and went out for dinner.

At first glance, Merlin looked as if he might have jumped right out of the pages of Easy Rider magazine. He was middle-aged and of average height. A biker's beanie adorned his shaved head, and a graying Fu Manchu mustache framed a frequent smile. A cherry-flavored Swisher Sweet often bounced in his lips as he rarely found himself at a loss for chatter. On the day we met, he wore a black sleeveless tee shirt and a faded pair of jeans, which held the dangling chain of a biker's wallet. As truckers go, Merlin looked to be in pretty good physical condition. He had, thus far, avoided falling victim to trucker's physique. His gregarious and playful personality made it impossible not to like him on first impression. Since I also fashioned myself with a shaved head, this evoked immediate joking from Calvin and Mona.

"You guys are going to look like the Cue Ball Brothers going down the road!" they laughed.

Our first delivery would be to Helena, Montana, but Merlin's truck required repairs that would not be completed for twenty-four hours. In order to make Helena on time, we would have to drive as a team rather than trainer/trainee. We slept in the truck that night and, although the Freightliner was much roomier than my old Mack, it still didn't compare to a real bed.

Merlin and I ate breakfast in the cafeteria the next morning where we watched the rain pelt down in violent torrents. He asked if I would prefer a day or night shift, and I opted for the night shift since I had no desire to familiarize myself with a new vehicle in the midst of a mad rainstorm. I did not know whether I'd be able to sleep in a moving truck, but I discovered that fatigue, in the proper amount, could inspire me to sleep anywhere. We drove through Nebraska and Wyoming and made it to Helena on time.

Helena was formerly called *Crabtown* after John Crab, one of the "Four Georgians" who discovered gold along Last Chance Creek. Helena's main street is named Last Chance Gulch and follows the path of the original creek through the historic downtown district.[15]

Since I was exhausted when we arrived at the customer, Merlin mercifully agreed to do all of the backing. I didn't know it at the time, but Merlin would continue to run us as a team. By week's end, we had logged over seven thousand miles. Merlin became giddy and challenged me to "break the record" next week. I told him that I would probably be more enthusiastic about all this mileage if I weren't doing it for trainee's pay while I was making him wealthy. After that, he frequently offered to buy my dinner.

In fairness, however, Merlin spent a lot of time up front with me while I was driving. He required little sleep, and he usually remained up front for three or four hours after his shift to offer training and to shoot the breeze. Merlin had been on the road for twenty-five years, and I was confident that he could help me to polish the skills I had, and learn the ones I had yet to acquire.

From Montana, we would deliver small arms ammunition to Prairie du Chien, Wisconsin. Although this is a French name meaning *Prairie of the Dog*, Merlin referred to it as "Prairie Chicken." I drove through Montana, across South Dakota, and into Minnesota before I ran out of hours.

On the first night, my gear shifting had been pretty good. On the second night, it was almost as if I had forgotten how. I was grinding gears like a little old lady in a Dodge Dart, and often missing them on the first attempt. This trend continued through the third day until I finally showed signs of improvement on the fourth day.

From Wisconsin, we got a load of sporting goods going to North Platte, Nebraska. North Platte is home to Bailey Yard, the world's largest rail yard. During the 1930's, high crime rates and corruption caused North Platte to be infamously known as Little Chicago. The morally dubious business operations soon captured the interest of real mobsters back east, and representatives from crime families in New York and Chicago were sent to get a piece of the action.[16] I feared that Merlin might have a desire to "whack" me after I made my first attempt to back into a dock when we arrived at the customer. I finally got the job done but suffice it to say—it wasn't pretty.

When Merlin coached me, he had a tendency toward overzealousness—sometimes to the point where I perceived it as yelling. I had already politely asked him not to yell at me, and he explained that he did not mean to be yelling; he just had a high-strung personality. I knew this to be true, so I took him at his word. After that, he made an effort to tone down his passion and I, in turn, made an attempt to overlook it when it spilled out.

Despite the minor disagreements we'd had, I found Merlin to be an otherwise congenial person. He had a terrific sense of humor, and he provided a constant source of entertainment. During our time together, we shared one another's life stories, and I came to respect him and consider him a friend. We discussed everything from fishing and poker to beer and women, to Nietzsche and Kierkegaard. While Merlin did not have an academic background in philosophy, he had a relentlessly inquisitive mind, and he never seemed to tire of discussing it. It gave him infinite delight when he felt that he had gotten the best of me on a philosophical point.

After North Platte, to my delight, we got a load going to Athens, Georgia. This would give me the opportunity to stop by my house to check on Kitty, and to pick up my permanent driver's license. It had been necessary to have a Hazmat endorsement added to my license before going to work for this company, and I was currently driving with a temporary license on which the expiration date rapidly approached. Unfortunately, the Georgia run was not to be.

Merlin found out that Mona had fallen ill on the road and had to go home for medical tests. He called Calvin and offered to swap loads so he could be home with his wife. So, we switched loads with Calvin at a truck stop and reversed course toward Green River, Wyoming. I was disappointed that I wouldn't get to stop at home, but I could not fault Merlin for being a good friend to Calvin.

Before this, I had never been out west other than for Navy boot camp in San Diego. I was enthralled by the majesty of Big Sky country. The sunsets out here looked as if they had been painted directly from the hand of God. As we traveled along I-80, the vast open spaces of Wyoming would be suddenly interrupted by a series of multi-colored buttes. Bearing witness to this kind of breathtaking beauty made me feel that I had finally discovered what trucking was <u>supposed</u> to be like. I didn't know it at the time, but this feeling would plant the seeds for a future decision. Prior to this, I had never seen a tumbleweed blow across the interstate but, I not only saw one, I also got a piece of it lodged in the grill.

We made our delivery to Green River and then got a load that we dropped in Ottawa, Illinois. From there, we got a load going to Kansas City. This meant a respite at Merlin's house in Cross Timbers, Missouri for a 34-hour restart.

Cross Timbers is a tiny rural town in Hickory County, Missouri that boasts a population of one hundred and eighty-five, but it does have its own Post Office. Merlin joked that the only thing you can buy in Cross Timbers is a stamp. When we got there, I saw that it wasn't much of an exaggeration.

I met Merlin's family, his wife, Rita, his two daughters, Amy and Melissa, and his son, Ronny. His other son was away serving in the Air Force. All of his children were young adults, so everyone spent the first night playing poker and consuming various…consumables. It was my first time playing Texas Hold 'em, but I wasn't fortunate enough to have beginner's luck—I was the first one busted.

Next morning, I walked to the town square where the Cross Timbers auction was being held. A fast-talking auctioneer attempted to sell what looked like a horde of junk, so it didn't take long for my interest to wane. Merlin had wanted to be home for the auction to bid on a piece of land where he could park his truck. I returned to Merlin's house and left him to his business.

When I returned, an equipment malfunction in the restroom left me in an unenviable position. After attending to my business, I exited the bathroom and coyly entered the living room where Rita, Amy, and Melissa sat. There are certain questions that one hates to pose when they are a guest in someone else's house, but I found myself in the unfortunate position of being forced to ask one of them. I reluctantly turned to Rita and delivered my embarrassing query.

"Do you have a plunger?'"

Week 17 and 18: Tragedy in Cross Timbers

After our 34-hour restart, Merlin and I made our first delivery to Memphis and then got a load going to Rome, Georgia. This meant that I would finally be able to stop in Scottsboro to pick up my permanent license and check on Kitty. Merlin and I continued to grow closer and I was beginning to see that his mad methods were actually making me a better driver. My confidence and skills were growing with each passing day.

We spent the night at my house in Scottsboro. Kitty and I had a joyous reunion. She was almost as happy to see me as I was to see her. When I gave her the expected jar of homecoming baby food, Merlin scrunched up his brow in confusion and said, "Baby food for a cat?"

I guess he just didn't understand the bond.

I hated to leave Kitty alone again, but I tried to appease her with all the Chicken & Cheese flavored *Whisker Lickin's* she could eat before Merlin and I set out for Rome the next morning. We had a bit of trouble finding our customer, but Merlin seemed to possess a sixth sense that I lacked.

From Georgia, we rolled across the United States: Minooka, Illinois; Kansas City; Grantsville, Utah; and Topeka, Kansas. I especially enjoyed the splendor of the snow-capped peaks of the Rockies in Utah and the colorful stony-ridged cliffs along the interstate. Merlin and I were already making plans to go fishing in Colorado together and, by this time, being on the road with him was just plain fun. I had even begun to toy with the idea of running nationally instead of regionally. This felt like what I had imagined trucking to be. I was eager to get out on my own and start earning decent money, but I knew I'd miss Merlin when my training was complete.

After we arrived in Topeka, Merlin stuck his head through the sleeper curtain with the obligatory *"Are we there yet?"* before I was forced to deal with a security guard who wore an inferiority complex as distasteful as the cheaply-embroidered cloth security badge on his uniform. He haughtily wielded the power of his synthetic patch as if it gave him carte blanche to be rude, obnoxious, and condescending. Nonetheless, we endured the wrath of Deputy Doofus and got a load going back to Memphis. Once again, we would stop at Merlin's house in Cross Timbers for another restart. We stopped along the way for food and beverages, and all was set for another fun-filled revelry.

Just as before, Merlin immediately fired up his riding mower and sputtered about the yard as soon as we arrived. He spun around on the mower with the joy of a child, and I could not conceal a smile watching the sun reflect off his shaved dome as the mower spewed its mulch. When the task was complete, I teasingly asked him if he had a license for that thing.

"In this yard, I'm legal to drive anything I want!" he replied with an ear-to-ear grin.

About that time, Merlin's son, Ronny, whirled into the back yard on a newly acquired motorcycle. Father and son stepped off to discuss the finer points of biking for a few moments, and then Merlin mounted the bike to go out for a test drive. He came back a few minutes later, and we went inside for dinner. Then, I decided to take a walk up to the town square. A craving for Boston cream donuts had penetrated my defenses of willpower earlier today, so I figured a little caloric burning wouldn't hurt.

When I returned to the house after my walk, everyone was gone, so I went out to the truck for a snack and to stretch out on the sleeper to relax for a while. Less than five minutes had elapsed when a loud banging on the window interrupted my respite.

"Rick! Rick!" cried a voice, which I discerned to be that of Rita.

I opened the door to reveal a distraught face with a pair of bloodshot eyes and cheeks lined with streaming tears. "Merlin's been airlifted to Springfield," sobbed Rita with a quivering lip, "he was in a motorcycle wreck."

Oh my God! I thought. *Airlifted? This can't be good.*

It wasn't.

There was not enough room for me to ride in the car with them, but Kathy, the lady with whom Rita was riding, gave me her husband's phone number. I had met Gerald, Kathy's husband, earlier when Merlin and I first arrived in Cross Timbers. Merlin referred to him as "the nature guy" because of Gerald's affinity for picking wild mushrooms.

Gerald was an apple-cheeked man with a face marked by laugh lines and partially covered by a thick, white Santa Claus beard. His cheerful and untroubled nature was often replaced with a look of concern as we rode together to Cox Medical Center South in Springfield where they'd taken Merlin. A congregation of family and friends had already banded together in the waiting room by the time we arrived. It was obvious from the outset that many people shared a love and concern for Merlin and, after having spent an all-too-brief time with him, it wasn't hard to understand why.

Merlin's injuries were severe. His ankle was mangled to the point where doctors were unsure whether he would be able to keep his foot. He had a broken arm and four broken ribs, and there was hemorrhaging in his brain from a blow to the head.

As of the next morning, the news was cautiously hopeful. Although Merlin had not regained consciousness, the doctors said that his brain had not swollen, and his ankle had not gotten any worse. The challenge would be to keep infection at bay.

I joined in the prayer circle among family and friends at the hospital and I was deeply touched by the outpouring of love and emotion on Merlin's behalf. I vowed to pray for him until the crisis had passed. While my concerns were with Merlin and his family, I also had to consider my own matters. Now, I was without a trainer and stranded in rural Missouri.

I called the company from the hospital, but the conversation offered no immediate solution. After sleeping badly, I called again the next morning and got better results. The company sent another driver to pick up our Memphis load, and they told me to call back in the morning for further instructions.

Merlin's family was being extremely helpful and accommodating to me during this trying time, but I did not want to impose myself for any longer than necessary. I was, however, doing my best to do what was needed of me. I made all of the arrangements to get our load headed to Memphis, and I gave the company all the details of this situation to the best of my knowledge. The neighbors in this small community also joined together to lend support. Gerald even brought over a heaping plate lunch for me…mushrooms included. I had not gotten over the sensation of being shell-shocked over this turn of events, but I resolved to deal with it to the best of my ability…and keep praying for Merlin.

On Monday, I got word from the company to bring Merlin's truck to the Kansas City terminal. His belongings onboard the truck represented a significant chunk of his life, and it required the better part of three hours to get it all unloaded. After that, I made a sandwich and left a note for Merlin and his family. Everyone here had been so kind to me, and so trusting of me. After all my years in the disingenuous world of the television business, I suppose I had forgotten the simplicity, humanity, and innocence of rural life and genuine people. Despite the tragic circumstances, it had been a heartwarming experience and an absolute joy to be around these folks.

I climbed into the barren husk that had been Merlin's truck, and left to pick up the empty trailer that the other driver had parked on a dusty county road. As I hooked up and left, I got my bearings crossed and turned the wrong way. There was nowhere to turn around on the tiny road, so my first solo trip began by taking the truck down narrow, winding dirt roads in the sticks of Missouri while praying for a paved highway to emerge.

I spotted a rustic house with a chain-link fence around it, where a stout woman in coveralls tended to a garden in the front yard. I stopped to ask for directions back to US65. As she spoke, her instructions were frequently drowned out by an angry, barking pit bull that was making a valiant effort to scale the structure that separated me from its bared teeth. The lady probably saw me for what I was, a lost rookie, while the pit bull hungrily inspected me as a menu item. I was relieved when I got the information I needed, over the furious growls of the animal, and got on my way to Kansas City.

I had no further problems for the remainder of the trip, and I spent the night in the truck at the Kansas City terminal. It felt odd and empty in there without Merlin. I chuckled as I recalled one aspect of his company that I wouldn't miss. I would not miss his dynamic snoring. When he was in rare form, the resonance of his nasal melody resembled what I'd imagine a rhinoceros farting into a tuba would sound like. I already missed him.

My phone rang at 8am the next morning. The main terminal in Lincoln informed me that my new trainer was already in Kansas City. I went over to meet him and immediately began transferring my belongings to his truck.

My new trainer's name was Brian, and my first impression of him left an uncertain feeling. He looked to be in his fifties, and his stoic behavior was accompanied by a disheveled appearance. A graying mustache complimented a tanned, furrowed face, and a dingy baseball cap covered a crop of thinning brown hair. His angular frame supported a plump paunch, which bulged just enough for him to frequently utilize it as a mouse pad for his computer. I introduced myself and reached out to shake his hand. The limber, droopy grip that he offered in return suggested that he wasn't exactly delirious with excitement to receive my company.

As I loaded my gear into the truck, it appeared in equal disarray. Wires and cables were strewn about like an angel-hair pasta dish gone horribly wrong, and there was precious little storage space for my gear. At this point, I really didn't know what to make of this guy.

Unlike Merlin, Brian would not accept team runs, which meant that I would do most of the driving. My shifting had evolved to an acceptable level, but I still hadn't quite got the hang of "slip-shifting," or changing gears without using the clutch. So, I was still using the "double-clutch" method as we rolled out of the terminal on our way to Minneapolis, Minnesota.

The more that Brian and I talked as we went down the road, the more I began to see that what I had initially perceived as stoic was, instead, an easygoing facet of his personality. When I told him that I was here to learn from him rather than to try and prove that I already knew everything, this softened his defenses and he became quite talkative. He acknowledged that many drivers with a small amount of prior experience come in thinking that they already know everything. He had been afraid that I was one of them. After a bit of communication, I found Brian very easy to get along with. It appeared that each of our initial perceptions had been off the mark.

When we shut down for the evening, Brian proved his prowess with a travel stove by whipping up a mouth-watering dish of jambalaya. It was so tasty that it inspired me to get a stove of my own when I was assigned to my truck. Up to this point, I had been eating a fare of sandwiches and cold canned goods on the road. With a little extra effort and planning, I saw that you could actually have a *real* meal out here without paying for one in a truck stop restaurant. We would enjoy such dishes as Yankee Pot Roast, baked chicken and vegetables, turkey and rice, and jambalaya with Italian sausage. I had not eaten this well on the road since I'd been out here. I knew that some drivers carried microwaves on board, but I had never been willing to buy one of the expensive power inverters needed to operate one. Besides, there hadn't been room for a microwave in my old Mack. The little lunch box oven seemed to be the solution I was looking for.

We arose early the next morning and I had my first experience of Minneapolis driving.

Detour: Drivers versus Dispatchers?

Unlike the National fleet, the upside of being on a regional or local fleet is that you work, primarily, with one dispatcher. At least, that was true of the company I worked for. The downside is that this dispatcher might be difficult to work with. My experience in trucking has afforded me the opinion that the relationship between drivers and dispatchers is often of the love/hate variety—minus the love in several cases.

I believe the "*us versus them*" attitude stems from a lack of communication between drivers and dispatchers and a lack of understanding of one another's respective roles. I will be the first to admit that this consideration did not factor in my thinking early on. In many cases, an unhappy driver is simply the result of a lack of understanding of the office structure, policies, and the role of key people in the company. Two-way communication and mutual respect are imperative in a successful relationship between drivers and dispatchers, and it is necessary for the retention of experienced drivers to a company.

I failed to understand early in my trucking career that most dispatchers do not willingly aspire to villainous acts. The role of a freight dispatcher, especially in a large company, is an incredibly stressful job. Not only are they juggling the scheduling and progress of multiple trucks while continually resolving problems that emerge, they listen to the gripes of drivers on a daily basis. On top of this, precious few dispatchers are afforded proper stress management training. They are, generally, just thrown into the fire.

I believe an essential ingredient in a driver's success and happiness with a company starts with an understanding of, and communication with, his or her dispatcher. Nobody will have more influence on a driver's success than a dispatcher.

Most dispatchers identify poor communication as a primary cause of stress. Many drivers are quick to classify their dispatcher as a nincompoop, but are slow to seek two-way communication. As a driver, I know that the stresses of the road are numerous and real, and it is easy to get caught up in a self-centered mindset. I once even heard another driver comment, "The dispatcher is there to serve us…not the other way around."

Wrong! The dispatcher is there to serve the needs of the company.

Dispatching is a sedentary job but, having worked in a sedentary job, I know that mental and emotional stress can be just as debilitating as physical stress. This pressure leads many dispatchers, like drivers, to have an abysmal diet. Fast food, fried foods, and vending machine junk are often the standard fare seen in a dispatch office. At my former company, I once noticed a bulk tub of antacid tablets nestled snugly in the bottom drawer of my driver manager's desk. I have little doubt that I caused him to gobble some of them.

A dispatcher is under constant pressure from his terminal manager to move freight, and a terminal manager is under constant pressure from company executives to keep his terminal productive and running smoothly. Unfortunately, this often translates into a perception of an uncaring or unfeeling attitude in the eyes of the driver. A driver needs to educate himself on the basic operations of his company and on the roles of some of the key people in it. Nevertheless, as I said before, communication is a two-way street. The company, as a whole, needs to afford greater consideration toward the drivers—the lifeblood of the industry.

When I was in orientation at my former company, a newly hired dispatcher was inserted into the class with the drivers. When one of the drivers asked him why he was there, he replied,

"They wanted to put me in here so I could learn what you guys go through."

I was fresh out of CDL School, so I did not respond but, among the experienced drivers, a number of lower jaws collectively banged to the floor.

"If you want to learn what we go through," barked a shocked driver, "you need to go on the road with us. You're not going to learn anything sitting in here."

This was a prime example of "Let's watch a rodeo to know the cowboy life" thinking. You might as well watch a Three Stooges skit with Larry, Curly, and Moe playing the roles of soldiers in the Allied Forces to understand the nature of World War II. A real cross-familiarization program would consist of ride-alongs by dispatchers, and time spent in a dispatch office by drivers. I can only assume that most companies do not consider this to be a cost-effective practice but, in adhering to this line of thinking, they fail to recognize that familiarity breeds mutual respect.

Drivers and dispatchers, by virtue of their mutual ignorance of one another's working environment, each formulate strong opinions about the other. It doesn't matter if these views are correct, but by allowing them to propagate and take hold, it often creates a negative work environment. In many cases, a negative relationship between a driver and a dispatcher is the fault of neither of them. Rather, companies that are content to maintain a revolving door policy concerning its drivers deserves the finger of blame.

It never ceases to amaze me that many trucking companies cannot grasp the concept that drivers desire to be treated like a human beings rather than a vehicle numbers on a computer monitor. It is easy to forget that those numbers represent men and women who have lives and families outside of that truck, and they deserve to live them like anyone else. Do they really think that an OTR national driver can cram his personal life into three or four days a month at home?

Repeatedly, home time is cited as the number one reason why drivers quit. Recruiters often misrepresent the amount of home time that a driver will be afforded, and this dishonesty often leads to short-term employment. Nothing makes me feel more insignificant than a company giving me the impression that a load of freight is more important than I am.

A standard industry response for not getting a driver home when requested might be: "Freight is slow. Be flexible until the freight situation allows us to route you home."

The person or people who provide such a response spend(s) an average of 420-480 hours per month at home with their families. An OTR national driver spends an average of 72-96 hours per month at home. How much do they expect us to "flex?" Most of us are already at the breaking point at the time our home request rolls around. If a company is unable to follow through on its promise of home time, it should not offer it as a hiring incentive. I am willing to be a team player, but when the company has little or no consideration for my need to live a personal life outside their truck, that company can summarily kiss my rigid and inflexible ass.

Dispatchers and trucking companies need to understand that drivers are real, live human beings rather than just a truck number. Likewise, drivers need to know that dispatchers and managers have a particular job to do, and they are under a lot of pressure just as we are. A dispatcher has the unenviable task of piecing together an enormous jigsaw puzzle, and the driver is only privy to his or her small portion of it. While communication will not resolve all issues, it will go a long way toward providing a better understanding and developing mutual respect. It is not a matter of kissing the dispatcher's or manager's butt, it is just a matter of opening a line of professional communication with them.

Week 19: Life with Brian

The docking procedure in Minneapolis required a blindside backing maneuver in extremely tight quarters. Thankfully, Brian did this one for me, but even he utilized me as a guide and got out to look several times. This was a very tricky operation, but he pulled it off brilliantly. My initial misgivings notwithstanding, Brian was showing me that he was a darned good driver and a superb trainer to boot.

On a personal level, I may have felt a deeper kinship with Merlin, but his training methods were often high-strung, and could sometimes make me nervous to the point of getting pissed off. In contrast, Brian's method was laid back and systematic. He never once made me nervous or tense. I came to appreciate Brian as both a trainer and as a person.

As advertised, I did almost all of the driving for the remainder of the week. We went to Eau Claire, Wisconsin and then Ottumwa, Iowa, home of the fictional character, Radar O'Reilly from the television series *MASH*. Ottumwa is known for its many historic locations in the downtown area. In the central downtown area, the *Canteen Lunch in the Alley* restaurant has been a stopping point for Ottumwa residents since the 1920's. Roseanne Barr's "loose meat sandwich" restaurant on the television series, *Roseanne* was based on Ottumwa's Canteen Lunch in the Alley.[17]

After Ottumwa, we went to Cedar Rapids, Iowa followed by Salt Lake City, Utah. Since Brian lives in Ogden, he planned to spend three days at home. So, we dropped our load at the Salt Lake City terminal and Brian put me up in an Ogden motel room for three days.

Originally named Fort Buenaventura, the city of Ogden was the first permanent settlement by people of European descent in the Utah region. In November of 1847, the Mormon settlers purchased Fort Buenaventura for $1,950. Ogden sits at the base of the Wasatch Mountains, and I took the opportunity afforded by my three-day respite to walk around and explore the beautiful sights. Ogden has also served as a filming location for a variety of movies and television series, although Ogden residents may or may not wish to acknowledge that *Dumb and Dumber* was filmed here.[18]

Two more weeks remained before my training with Brian was complete. I talked to Ringo again over the weekend and he said that Kitty was as "ornery" as ever. She missed her daddy.

Although I enjoyed my exploration of Ogden, I was antsy by the third day. I was ready to get back on the road to complete my training.

Week 20 and 21: No Trucks Allowed!

Brian picked me up at the motel Wednesday morning for our first delivery to Foster City, California in the Bay area, with two stop-offs along the way. I enjoyed sights that I had never seen as we drove along the Salt Flats of Utah on I-80. The flat, white surface of the Salt Flats looked eerily like an alien planet. We encountered a bevy of bugs in Nevada that prompted two stops to clean them off for visibility purposes. We shut down for the night in Mill City, Nevada where the obligatory casino was right next to the truck stop.

I have never been much for gambling, but Brian gave me a ten-dollar token and told me to go have fun. To my utter surprise, I won forty-three dollars on a slot machine on the first spin. The lure of the one-armed bandit beckoned strongly, but I decided to quit while I was ahead. I gave Brian half my winnings and walked away with a bit of change to jingle in my pockets.

At the casino, we ran into a guy who called himself "The Captain," whose endless seafaring tall tales were about as captivating as a barnacle-encrusted poop deck. If I had been at sea with him, I would have been tempted to chain an anchor around my ankle and toss it over the starboard side to end my suffering. I thought he would never shut up. My left knee (and my resolve) was beginning to fail me while we stood as unwilling receptacles of his infinite blathering. When we were finally able to cast off, Brian and I bought some ice cream and went back to the truck to call it a night.

Next day, we drove past many Nevada gold mines along the interstate. Nevada gold mines are one of the largest sources of gold in the world. Seventy-nine percent of all the gold mined in the United States comes from the mines of Nevada.[19]

Having never been in this part of the country, I was basking in the beauty of the west. The California wine country was breathtakingly gorgeous, but the hills were slow and tedious in a truck hauling over 40,000 pounds. The downside of seeing all these beautiful sights was the lack of time to stop and enjoy them in all their glory. We were truckers—not tourists.

I had a near miss at our first stop-off location in Mountain View, California when I ran up on another vehicle too fast and had to slam the brakes. It was the first time I had caused Brian to scream, "Oh shit! Look out!" Fortunately, I avoided disaster and apologized to Brian as he checked his pulse, and I checked my pants.

By this time, I was convinced that Brian was the right trainer for me. Aside from the previous event, he was laid-back, calm, and offered constant encouragement. For instance, when I got tense in preparation for a tight backing maneuver, he stopped me for a moment and said something like: "Rick, you have the ability to do this; you just have to believe you can do it."

Over the past few weeks, having witnessed other drivers struggle with backing in docks and at truck stops, I saw that I was actually better than some of them. However, I still could not seem to get past a foreboding sense of dread when I had to do it. Brian assured me that the fear would pass with time. I hoped he was right.

When we arrived at our customer in Mountain View, Brian wanted me to park behind the building for the night since the client would not accept delivery until the next morning. In order to point the trailer toward the dock, I had to pull out into the busy street, back up, and turn around while Brian placed cones on the road and played the role of faux traffic cop to deter traffic during the precarious maneuver. I managed to pull it off, but it was a nerve-wracking experience.

Mountain View is one of the major cities that make up Silicon Valley, [20] but I would not have known this by virtue of our spending the night in an alley there. When we were settled, Brian unveiled his travel stove to play the role of chef, and I got out of the truck to perform my *Ten Dollar Workout*. I had purchased a silly set of bungee cords, for ten dollars, which was laughingly called an "Ultimate Travel Gym." Despite feeling like an idiot for paying ten bucks for something that probably cost no more than fifty cents to manufacture, it was better than nothing. Staying fit on the road is a tall order for anyone, but I was determined to try.

Next morning, I backed into the dock when the receiving crew arrived and went inside to forage for a badly-needed cup of coffee. Our next stop-off was in Redwood City, California before going to our final destination in Foster City. I would dub this *Hell Day* because I had to perform two blindside backs along with three other backing maneuvers in very tight quarters. I was worn out by day's end, and Brian said he was going to start calling me "Blindside." I was happy to have seen the Bay area for the first time, but I was ready to get out of California and start heading home. I was pleasantly surprised to discover that Brian was also a cat lover who had three of his own. He invited me to bring Kitty along the next time we got to Scottsboro, so I was eager to get home and rescue my feline friend from her solitude.

As I lamented over my inconsistency in backing, Brian shared a story of when he accidentally turned into a residential area and was forced to attempt circling the block to get out. As he navigated the narrow street and fought to avoid tearing down stop signs and fire hydrants, he was unable to steer clear of a lilac bush in someone's yard. As his drive tires mangled the lilac bush, a little old blue-haired lady toddled toward his truck with fire in her eyes, and a broom clutched firmly in her hands. With a fury that belied her age, she angrily swatted at Brian's truck with the broom as she screamed, "No trucks allowed! No trucks allowed!" Despite Brian's efforts to assure the lady that he was doing his best to exit the premises, she continued the relentless attack on his truck and maintained her insistence that there were "No trucks allowed!"

He told of another time when he awakened abruptly from the sleeper berth with an unsettling sensation that the truck was rolling. In the frenzy of his mad scramble to the cab, he did not realize it when he snagged his underwear on a protruding object. As the fog of slumber evaporated, he discovered that he was standing there wearing nothing but his birthday suit. His next discovery was that a woman with a poodle on a leash had witnessed the entire event, and stood frozen in front of his truck wearing a wanton smile.

I think that everyone who has done this job has had a share of sticky and embarrassing moments. I have already had a few of my own.

Mercifully, Brian took over driving after Foster City because he knew I had been through the wringer. We picked up a load in West Sacramento and dropped it in Stockton. Then, we were off to Santa Clara and Fontana. I thought we would never get out of California, but we then got a load going to Menomonee Falls, Wisconsin. This would not take us past Scottsboro but, at least, it would get us headed back east.

We spent the next two days driving in the mountains and on the winding roads of Nevada, Arizona, and Colorado. We shut down at the Lincoln terminal on the third night where I called Rita again to check on Merlin. He had regained consciousness, but the fate of his mutilated ankle was still undetermined. The blow to his head had also prompted some memory loss. Rita told me that Merlin didn't even remember who I was.

We made it to Menomonee Falls on the fourth night and the docking maneuver, once again, would require a blindside approach. With Brian's help, old "Blindside" got the job done once again. After making the delivery the next morning, we got a load going to Fairburn, Georgia. This would finally allow me to stop by the house and get Kitty. I had a new lease on life now!

When I got home, Kitty's food dishes were empty and her water bowl was dry. I was none too happy with the twelve-year-old caretaker to whom I had entrusted this duty. I still paid the boy what I had promised, but his excuse that he'd lost the key did little to assuage my annoyance. I resolved that if I ever needed another cat-sitter, it would be a responsible adult.

None of that mattered now as Kitty was on board with us as we headed out for Fairburn, then Indianapolis and North Carolina. From there, we got a load going back to Ogden, Utah where Brian would take home time again. I would not be going that far though. The company sent word that my truck was waiting for me at the terminal in Cheyenne, Wyoming. My time with Brian was almost over. It was time to go solo again.

Week 22: Tastes Like Chicken!

Brian and I got to the terminal in Cheyenne on Wednesday. Brian assisted me in making the transition into my bright red Freightliner, and then it was time to part ways. I thanked him for being a good trainer and promised to stay in touch, and then he was off. Before leaving, he suggested I stay at the terminal overnight and postpone telling dispatch that I was ready for a load until the next morning. This seemed like a good idea. I needed to get a shower and pick up a few supplies from the nearby truck stop anyway. The only supplies I had were what I had brought along in a sea bag. I had no CB radio, no food…no anything. I needed to get home in order to outfit my truck properly.

After my shower, I had dinner at a truck stop restaurant and returned to the terminal in anticipation of enjoying the book I had been reading. I was irked to discover that I had left my only source of entertainment in Brian's truck. I went back to the truck stop and bought another book. Truck stops aren't known for stocking diverse selections of literature, but a *Gunsmoke* paperback about Marshall Dillon and Festus is better than nothing.

Next morning, I sent in a call that I was ready for my first load and, as it turned out, my load was already sitting in the terminal yard. All I had to do is hook up and go. This load would be going to Hermiston, Oregon.

Shit! I thought. *They're sending me the wrong way!*

I was assigned to the southeast regional Coca-Cola/Minute Maid fleet so, I assumed they would send me back east. However, this was a good run, so I did not offer any resistance. There was, nonetheless, another bug in the mix. The company wanted me to pick up a new trainee in Cheyenne and take him to the Salt Lake City terminal to meet his trainer. I was not thrilled with the idea of having a passenger when I had yet to familiarize myself with the truck, but I had no choice. The trainee's name was Jericho, who was a nice enough fellow, but I was anxious to get him to Salt Lake so I could be on my own.

I had a heavy load, so the going was slow on the mountain grades of Wyoming heading into Utah. At about the point where US 189 splits, I-80 offers up a triple helping of the main hills. This area is, collectively, known as "The Three Sisters."[21]

As fate would have it, I missed my exit to the terminal in Salt Lake and, thanks to Jericho's self-proclaimed knowledge of Salt Lake City, we took an unplanned tour that was long and painful. Fortunately, Jericho's trainer was already at the terminal when we arrived so, I helped him unload his gear from my truck, wished him well, and sent him on his way. My first assignment had been laden with a few potholes, but it was now complete. I spent the night at the terminal and got up early the next morning to continue the journey to Hermiston.

Hermiston is a small town located on the northeastern edge of Oregon in Umatilla County. The large watermelon slice painted on the *Welcome to Hermiston* sign indicates that the city is well known for the watermelons grown there.

The delivery to the Wal-Mart distribution center in Hermiston went smoothly. Afterward, I even managed to park like a pro at the crowded Pilot truck stop. For the next assignment, we would pick up a load in Auburn, Washington and deliver to Topeka, Kansas. Finally, we'd be pointed in the right direction.

Kitty was adjusting well to the roominess of the Freightliner. There was more space to move around than in the smaller cab of the Mack. She sometimes rode on the floor and in the sleeper berth but, usually, she planted herself beside me in the passenger's seat. Whenever I stopped and got up from the driver's seat, Kitty often usurped my throne and argued relentlessly about having to relinquish it back to me. This particular behavior had amused Brian when Kitty was riding in his truck.

The mountains and crystal clear lakes of Washington State were breathtaking, and we passed by many cyclists that were out for a brisk mountain ride. After picking up our load in Auburn, we spent the night at a truck stop/casino in Montana. I ordered a one-pound hamburger at a restaurant across the street but, despite my best effort to pack it away, I wasn't quite able to get the job done.

As we drove through Montana the next day, I saw a billboard advertising the *Testicle Festival*. This is an annual September event held at the Rock Creek Lodge, which is 20 miles east of Missoula along I-90. Merlin and I had passed this way when I was riding with him, and he touted the virtues of Rocky Mountain Oysters.

"They taste like chicken and shrimp," he revealed.

"If I get a craving for chicken and shrimp," I countered, "I'll have chicken and shrimp. You can have all the *cojones* you want!"

The motto of the festival is: *I had a ball at the Testicle Festival*. The delectable nuggets are billed as Montana Tendergroin. The annual celebration includes such festive events as a wet tee shirt contest for women, a hairy chest contest for men, and *Bullshit Bingo*, which offers a grand prize to the person who correctly predicts where a cow will empty its bowels.[22] It sounded like a lot of fun, well...except for eating the "oysters."

We passed through South Dakota, Iowa, and the corner of Nebraska to get to Kansas. Fortunately, the Payless distribution center was a place I'd already been when I was with Merlin, so I knew where it was. The delivery went fine, and then we picked up a load of dog food from Hill's Pet in Topeka. I had to back into a dock off the street while impatient four-wheelers waited on me, but I pulled it off nicely. This load would go to Lavergne, Tennessee and then, we would finally go home.

Along the way, the sun glared so badly in St. Louis that I could not see the signs. I considered myself lucky to get through there without being sidetracked. I had a bit of trouble finding the customer in Lavergne and, once I did, it proved to be an impossibly congested and compact area in which to maneuver. I had to back into a tiny slot just in order to turn around and back into a teeny one. When the task was complete, I went back to the TA where I had spent the previous night to debate my next action.

I was less than two hours from home, but I only had thirty minutes remaining on my logbook to legally drive. I was tempted to unplug the Qualcomm and go home, but I called Brian instead. He advised me to call the log department in Lincoln to see if they would authorize my trip home as personal vehicle usage. I did as he suggested, but they proved to be about as helpful as sandpaper on a hemorrhoid. I used my remaining thirty minutes to go to Love's in Christiana, Tennessee to park. I decided that I did not want to run illegally after my first solo week, so I stayed there until I was legal to drive again.

We left for Scottsboro at the stroke of midnight, and I could tell that Kitty sensed we were homeward bound. The Coca-Cola/Minute Maid regional fleet awaited us. What adventures lay ahead?

Week 23: Avian Droppings

The first week of the new fleet began with a pickup in Atlanta. This was the first time I'd taken a big truck beyond the hallowed barrier of the I-285 bypass. Commercial vehicles are not allowed into the inner sanctum of Atlanta unless they are on business. Ringo had warned me that if I ever went into Atlanta in a big truck, I had better have paperwork to prove I had business there.

The customer was easy to find and well organized, so I was out in a little over an hour and on my way to Orlando. I had purchased a copy of *Streets and Trips* mapping software for my laptop computer, so I don't know how I missed John Young Parkway when I got to Orlando. I turned around to get back on course, but my directions had given an incorrect street name for the entrance to the customer. By the time I realized the error, I had already passed by the gate. I'd have to go around the block to backtrack. The only problem was that the "block" I chose did not go all the way around; it was not a block at all. I found myself taking a scenic tour through one of Orlando's residential areas while strategically weaving to avoid low-hanging branches. I kept looking for the little old blue-haired lady with a broom to run out and remind me that there were "No trucks allowed!" By the time I fumbled my way back to the customer, I was an hour late for my appointment. It was not an auspicious beginning.

After waiting in line for three hours, I received my dock assignment. I was faced with the task of backing in between a shiny new Kenworth and an empty trailer. The dirt road in front of the docks was narrow, and there was a fence to the right which prevented maneuverability. I did my best, but even my most supreme effort resulted in repeatedly banging into the empty trailer on my blind side. I was trying very hard <u>not</u> to slam into the shiny new Kenworth. The receiving personnel at last took mercy and assigned me to an easier dock a little farther down. By the time I got to the dock, I was soaked with sweat—

partially from the unrelenting Florida heat, but mostly from the stress.

After Orlando, Kitty and I were off to Auburndale, Florida. I followed the company's directions, which took me down Route 559 south, and right through the heart of Auburndale. The city offered narrow, serpentine streets that caused my two amigos to shrink to the size of raisins. I made a firm decision to find an alternate route the next time.

When I got to the shipper, there was a problem with my pickup number, so I had to sit for almost an hour before it got straightened out. Then, I saw that my load was on a reefer trailer. I shook my head in bewilderment, thinking that the hurdle of another mistake now blocked my path.

Brian had given me the phone number of one of his former trainees, Tony. Tony had been working in the Coca Cola/Minute Maid fleet for over a year, and Brian thought he would be an excellent source of information. I had called Tony earlier to introduce myself, and he seemed like an affable fellow. On this day, I called him again to ask about the reefer trailer.

"Oh, that's not unusual," he said. "You'll get a reefer trailer sometimes, but it's not a reefer load."

It was nice of dispatch to tell me! With that cleared up, I hooked up to my reefer trailer and went to the terminal in Deland, Florida to spend the night and get a badly needed shower.

Deland was the first city in Florida to have electricity, [23] but I did not feel particularly "charged" when I got a first look at the terminal there. It paled in comparison to the palatial edifice in Lincoln. Nonetheless, it would provide sanctuary for the night.

The hot water felt like heavenly beads caressing my body as I stood in the shower, washing away the grit and grime of this punishing day. Maintaining personal hygiene on the road often required, both literally and figuratively, going the extra mile. I did my best to get a shower every other day but, when that was not possible, I settled for a "bird bath." A plastic wash basin with Johnson's baby wash and a bottle of No-Rinse shampoo was no substitute for a real shower, but it was certainly better than nothing. I quickly discovered that the expectation of a daily shower in OTR trucking is destined to meet with disappointment. This is not to say it is necessary to go around emanating body odor—it isn't! But to make deliveries on time, maximize working hours, and get a bit of rest in between, it is sometimes necessary to settle for an imperfect solution.

Another taboo among many drivers is whether or not to keep a "pee-jug" in the truck. When I rode with Ringo, he refused to do this and had nothing but derogatory reviews for those drivers who did. At the time, I wholeheartedly agreed with him. Keeping a pee jug in the truck was disgusting! However, after literally peeing my pants on two separate occasions, my uncompromising opinion began to soften. Now, if I had a nickel for every time I've put my pecker to a milk jug spout, well— let's just say I wouldn't have to worry about toll roads for a while. While I am still not a cheerleader for storing bodily fluids in the truck, it beats the heck out of peeing my pants!

I fueled at the terminal early the next morning and then set out for Blythewood, South Carolina. My confidence had been shaken by the debacle in Orlando, so it didn't help when I toppled over a stack of wooden pallets in Blythewood as I backed into the dock. I even exacerbated the error by running over and crushing some of them. My confidence was officially rattled, and the familiar thoughts of quitting began to emerge once again. I could not understand why this was so damned hard for me.

Mathematics can be thrown out the window when backing a big truck. No two backing maneuvers are ever the same. Sometimes, there is a large staging area to do a nice big setup, and sometimes there isn't. Sometimes, the setup is between two other trucks, and the target is not even visible to the driver. There are all sorts of contingencies that factor into a backing maneuver. What it boils down to is intuition, and that only comes with experience. Some drivers boast that they were *always* good at backing. I seriously doubt that a single driver exists who was capable of masterful backing early in his or her career. Nevertheless, my spirit was crushed as I left Blythewood.

We went back to Auburndale to pick up a load going to a Coca-Cola warehouse in Atlanta. I should not have been surprised to see that the Atlanta warehouse was a miserably crowded place with a miniscule docking area. I nervously backed in between two other trucks with, perhaps, two or three inches clearance on either side. After almost taking out the mirror of the truck on my blind side, I made it to the dock and fought the urge to puke as my heart raced in my rapid breathing made me lightheaded. I'd never had this many problems at my first company, but I'd never had to perform precision backing, at this level, in flatbed trucking. I was truly getting a trial by fire and, thus far, I had repeatedly burned the crap out of myself.

After that, we went back to the Coke syrup plant to pick up another load and then, mercifully, headed back to Scottsboro for a 34-hour restart. The first week on the Coke fleet left me feeling like I'd been chewed up by a meat grinder.

I dropped my loaded trailer at a Scottsboro truck stop in preparation to bobtail home. As I walked back to the cab, I felt a suspicious "plop" followed by a warm sensation on my left ear. After dropping my load at the truck stop, a passing bird dropped its load on me. It seemed like an appropriate exclamation point to this hellish week!

Week 24: Low Times in High Springs

We left for Tampa, Florida on Sunday and, mercifully, this week started out smoothly. After delivering in Tampa, we picked up a load in Auburndale to take to Atlanta. We spent the night at a Georgia rest area and got up at 3am to go to Atlanta.

I had been on the interstate for about fifteen minutes when another truck passed me in the hammer lane. He had gone only a few feet past when I heard a loud BANG! Rubber and debris flew from beneath his trailer and violently pelted my windshield. Just a few moments earlier, I had bemoaned the impossibility of finding a palatable cup of coffee at a rest area. Now, I didn't need one; I was awake!

I was going back to the Coca-Cola warehouse, the one with the tiny docks. My nightmare continued when I actually <u>did</u> ding the mirror of the truck on my blind side this time. I got out to assess the damage to find the other driver already out of his truck. He was a lanky, middle-aged man who wore an understandably sour look as he stared at his dented mirror while refusing to look at me. I surveyed both sides of the mirror and saw that the damage confined itself to a little ding on the back. I offered my sincere apologies and awaited a response, but the man continued to ignore my presence. He grimaced at the mirror as if it were covered in baboon excrement. I felt terrible, but with his refusal to reply, I simply returned to my truck.

A few minutes later, he walked up to my window and broke his vow of silence.

"Did you see my mirror?" he asked.

"Yes," I replied.

"I'm gonna have to replace that mirror," he added.

"So," I asked, "What do you want to do?"

"I'm gonna have to replace that mirror," he repeated.

There was no question in my mind that the functionality of the mirror had not been compromised, but if he wanted to replace it for cosmetic purposes, that was his prerogative. After all, the damage was because of my error.

"Okay," I said, "we can file an accident report and my company's insurance will take care of your damage."

At that, he just walked away. I then watched him exit the shipper with his paperwork and simply drive off. I never heard from him again.

Apparently, he expected me to just start throwing money at him. I acknowledged my error, and it made me sick to my stomach, but I wasn't about to give him carte blanche to my wallet. I was willing to make reparations through the proper channels, but I believe that he saw a golden opportunity for a quick buck. At any rate, this event caused the balance of my fragile confidence to teeter even more precariously to the "cow pie" side of the fence.

After this catastrophe, we picked up at the Coke syrup plant in Atlanta to deliver to Jacksonville. The problem was that it was scheduled for a 3am delivery, and I didn't have the hours left to do it. I alerted dispatch to this problem, and they instructed me to go ahead and pick it up; they would change the appointment time. This sounded reasonable, so I picked it up and went to the Pilot in Byron, Georgia to shut down for the night. Shortly after I arrived, I got a Qualcomm message from dispatch stating that the customer had to have this delivery by 3am. Since I was out of hours to drive, I told dispatch they'd have to assign another driver to this load if the appointment time could not be changed. Dispatch agreed to send another driver, so I unhooked from the trailer and parked the bobtail in the spot next to it in order to make the transition easier. Then, I went in the truck stop for a shower and came back to go to bed. I figured the other driver would wake me when he arrived.

I awoke a little before 2am, and no one had shown up for the load. I called dispatch to find out what was going on.

"You've been taken off this load. Another driver will be there in about an hour and a half to get it," said the dispatcher.

"Well," I replied, "the entire point of swapping this load was so it could be in Jacksonville by 3am. It's 2am now. What time is it going to be in an hour and a half?"

He took a moment to compute this mathematical conundrum and replied with, "Let me get back to you."

Ultimately, I was reassigned to the load and instructed to get it there as soon as possible.

I arrived in Jacksonville at 9am only to be told by the Receiving Department that they could not unload me until 10pm. I called dispatch again and now, they wanted me to take it to High Springs, Florida. Dispatch had fumbled, thrown an interception, and been tackled for a safety in the execution of this game plan. Unfortunately, I was the one suffering the hits from the big, ugly linebackers. I was ready to punt and go rub some dirt on my wounds.

As I drove to High Springs, the number of four-wheelers who hunkered down as they passed to peer up into my truck bewildered me. I wasn't sure what they expected to see, but I figured their curiosity should be rewarded with…something. I blew a nonpartisan kiss to both men and women as I met their gawks. I'm not sure all of them interpreted it in the benevolent manner it was intended, but at least they got the satisfaction of knowing their effort was not met with apathy.

In High Springs, I finally ridded myself of this cumbersome albatross of a load, and then I got a series of three eighty-eight mile runs from High Springs to Jacksonville and back. I called it *The Trifecta from Hell*. It was hot, sweaty work, and I wasn't making much money on these short runs.

It would only get worse. The hellish three-peat ended with me putting a ding on the left front fender of my truck while trying to back into a dock. I believe my exhaustion diminished my capacity to pay attention, but that's still no excuse. I should have stopped before I allowed them to push me that hard. Fortunately, the damage did not involve another vehicle, and it was minor, but it was still noticeable. I had no choice but to report it to the Accident Department. I wondered what the hell was happening to me. I had made a lot of backing errors lately. My concern, however, rapidly morphed into indifference. I was so exhausted, I just didn't care.

After getting some rest, I agreed to take a weekend run to Lewisville, Texas instead of going home. After the Trifecta from Hell, I needed the money. I spent the night at the TA in Baldwin, Florida and set out on Saturday morning. I made it all the way to Talluah, Louisiana for the night. It had been a smooth day for a change.

Detour: Fitness, Hygiene, and Diet on the Road

Based on its research, the Transportation Research Board (TRB) says that the obesity in trucking is rampant. In response to the research, the Associated Press notes that many truckers do not wear seat belts because their stomachs get in the way; one in four have sleep apnea, and half of all truckers smoke compared to about one-fifth of all Americans.[24] All of these are risk factors for high blood pressure, heart disease, and diabetes. New studies reveal that truck drivers top the list of the most obese groups of workers in the United States.[25] Apparently, trucking poses a challenge for a healthy lifestyle. Dr. Martin Moore-Ede, a Toronto researcher, claims that truck drivers live ten to fifteen years less than the average North American male. Is there really anything a trucker can do to battle against a lifestyle that is not conducive to healthy living?

Trucking does not compare to an ordinary job. An OTR trucker does not have the option of hitting Gold's Gym after work every day, and few appear to have taken the advice of Chuck Norris with the purchase of a Total Gym. While there is a handful of drivers who pay attention to their health, the majority is among the unhealthiest eaters on the planet.

There are many reasons for the lack of healthy habits on the road. For a National driver, spending three to six weeks (or more) living in a truck simply has a way of chipping away resolve. After working fourteen hours, it is often difficult to muster the motivation to prepare a healthy meal. Fatigue and stress can highlight the appeal of comfort food in a restaurant. After veering off the path of healthy eating on the road, I can attest to the difficulty of getting back on track. Boredom and loneliness are the perfect scapegoats for an unhealthy meal or snack.

Author's Note: Fortunately, most major truck stops now offer fresh fruit, fresh salads, and more healthy meal and snack options than in years past. Eating healthy on the road is still a herculean task, but there are better options than there used to be.

While it may not be possible to regularly get a gym-quality workout on the road, some drivers take a creative approach to avoid the dreaded trucker's physique. A Wisconsin driver decided to start a walking routine. Instead of waiting around for his truck to be unloaded, he walked a mile or so into the nearest town. It is also a good idea to park at the back of a truck stop. This forces additional walking in the course of a typical day. Another driver I met stored a fold-up bicycle in his truck. Not only did it give him an enjoyable way to stay fit, it provided added mobility during downtime. It obviously worked for him, as he was lean and muscular. Also, some travel centers, like TA, have added fitness rooms and wellness programs to make it a little easier for drivers who care about their health.

The only limit to finding ways to stay fit on the road is the driver's creativity. I have seen a driver skipping rope at a truck stop, and another pumping iron on a weight bench beside his truck. Personally, I carry a set of dumbbells and resistance bands on the road, and I walk as much as I can. When I can't walk, I use a portable stepper that I store in the sleeper berth. It cost about fifty bucks. I generally prepare my own meals, but I sometimes fall victim to an insatiable craving for the greasy fare of the road. The best advice for any driver is to cook most meals in the truck, avoid fast foods and buffets, and exercise for at least a few minutes a day. Even Bojangles chicken, my personal weakness, seems less appealing when I watch a driver, with belly fat hanging almost to his knees, waddle toward the truck stop after having parked as close to the buffet as humanly possible.

Personal hygiene is another issue that proves challenging for some drivers. While there are those who swear they shower daily, I find it impractical to attempt a daily shower on the road. While it is theoretically possible, the sacrifice of sleep time would seem to outweigh the positives. My personal goal is to get a "real" shower every other day while settling for a quick wipe down with baby wipes on subsequent days. For me, this is a more practical goal that is usually attainable. When that isn't possible, I keep a large plastic bowl that can be filled with water and used as a wash basin for a sponge bath. I also have a bottle of No Rinse shampoo on board that serves as an alternative to the real thing in a pinch. There's really no excuse for a driver to go around emanating body odor.

The major truck stop chains are, ordinarily, good about providing clean shower facilities. With the purchase of fuel, the driver gets a free shower. Among the nicest shower facilities I have encountered is at the Bosselman Travel Center in Grand Island, Nebraska. They are always clean, and they are almost large enough for a three-on-three basketball game. As an added touch, the staff leaves a pair of Hershey's kisses for the driver.

On the opposite end of the spectrum, I have encountered shower facilities that reflected a lower standard of work ethics. The most disgusting shower I ever saw was at an independent truck stop in Winnie, Texas. Used towels lay askew, and I would have bet that the shower's last cleaning occurred during the Bill Clinton administration. I asked for my money back and took a bird bath in the truck.

I have also seen drivers who neglect oral hygiene. It never ceases to amaze me that while all major trucking companies offer dental plans, I see too many drivers with missing or disgusting teeth. I admit that it can be challenging to keep a medical or dental appointment, but I would take time off work, or even quit, before I'd let my teeth rot and fall out. I believe the majority of truckers care about personal hygiene, but a select few lend credence to the negative Hollywood stereotype.

More than once, I've watched a male driver flirt with a waitress or cashier at a truck stop while he is dirty and emanating a foul odor. His teeth (if he has them) are stained with coffee and nicotine and his butt crack peeks unassumingly above the back of his greasy Levi's. Still, he thinks he is God's gift to women. As one driver puts it, "People, in general, are either nasty or clean. Their occupation has little to do with it."

I tend to agree.

Week 25: Driver "Appreciation"

Sunday was another smooth day. I saw a goat casually munching grass on the shoulder of I-20 as I drove through Louisiana. You never know what you are going to see out here. I made a brief stop in Haughton, Louisiana, a small community just east of Shreveport, where my family lived for a couple of years when I was a teenager.

I hold fond memories of Haughton as it served as a mentor for my entry into the world of young adulthood. My best friend, Jay, and I used to camp out on weekends and climb atop abandoned oil derricks to look out upon the landscape and share our hopes and dreams.

I stopped at the TA in Terrell, Texas for the night and got a Qualcomm message shortly thereafter saying that a Driver Appreciation luncheon would be held at the Marietta, Georgia terminal next week. The company held a Driver Appreciation luncheon about once a month at various terminals, but it was simply luck of the draw for a driver to actually be able to attend. Over the course of two years, I attended exactly **zero** Driver Appreciation luncheons. I was out making money for the company while the office and maintenance staff "appreciated" me by stuffing their faces with turkey and dressing. While I don't mean to kick sand in the face of a generous gesture, the fact remains that it is the office and shop personnel who benefit most from Driver Appreciation luncheons. I think a more sincere gesture might be a Christmas bonus, or extra paid vacation days for drivers who stay out on major holidays or, at least, a restaurant certificate that the driver can actually use. If a company actually wants to show driver appreciation, there are better ways to do it than to throw a lunch that the vast majority of drivers can't attend.

A more telling indicator of driver appreciation occurred later in my career when I spent Christmas Day in my truck at a snowbound Columbus, Ohio terminal. Drivers were "appreciated" that day by being locked out of the terminal. I sent a message to the staff, which read:

Kudos to Columbus terminal for locking drivers out on Christmas Day. I guess you failed to take into account that while you are at home having dinner and exchanging gifts with your families, some of us are spending Christmas at a truck terminal in need of a shower. Ho, ho, freaking ho!

The delivery to Lewisville was satisfactory, and then we went to pick up another load from the terminal in Wilmer, Texas to deliver to Vonore, Tennessee. Wading through the molasses of Dallas morning traffic was about as fun as a habanero sauce enema.

After delivering to Vonore, I expected dispatch to send me home for my restart following the weekend Texas run. It turned out that "Bob," my dispatcher, had other ideas. After a heated rift with Dispatcher Bob, he finally allowed me to go home. I began to toy with the idea of leaving the Coke fleet and switching to the National fleet. The National fleet paid more, and Dispatcher Bob was something of a festering bag of shit.

I did not have adequate hours to drive to Scottsboro, so I spent the night at a dusty Tennessee truck stop in Niota called Crazy Ed's. I had an unexpectedly good meal at the restaurant inside, and it lifted my spirits a little. However, I found myself becoming disillusioned with trucking again. Had this whole thing just been a huge mistake?

Week 26: Frozen Orange Juice and Dispatcher Bob

We (Kitty and I) left on Friday since I took my restart in the middle of the week. We set out for Gadsden, Alabama to pick up our first load.

Gadsden boasts one of the biggest comeback stories in the nation. After the civil rights movement and the closing of most of the city's major industries in the 1970's and 80's, Gadsden was listed in a 1989 Rand McNally article as one of the "Seven Worst Cities to live in the United States." Spurred to action by these reports, redevelopment efforts earned Gadsden first place in the 2000 City Livability Awards Program.[26] Gadsden is also home to Judge Roy Moore. The "Praying Judge" made national headlines for his refusal to remove a monument of the Ten Commandments from the state courthouse while he was the elected Chief Justice of the Supreme Court of Alabama.

The directions to the shipper in Gadsden were a bit confusing, and I became sidetracked. Fortunately, I called the shipper and the man I spoke with was very helpful in providing verbal instructions. We picked up a load of metal coils in Gadsden that were going to Homerville, Georgia. These directions were also sketchy so I called Tony, Brian's former trainee, to ask if he had ever been there before. He said that he had, and he gave me better directions that turned out to be on the money. From Homerville, we went to High Springs, Florida for a load that was going to Dacula, Georgia.

Dacula began its history near the community of Chinquapin Grove.[27] Dacula has experienced immense growth over the past two decades, and many long-time Dacula residents say that they miss their "small one-light town."

I was fortunate to make it to the customer just in time because, if I hadn't, we would have been stuck in Dacula until Monday morning. Instead, we picked up another load in McDonough, Georgia that was going to Dunedin, Florida.

Getting to the customer in Dunedin was a challenge because we were forced to look for it in the midst of a violent rainstorm. Driving in an unfamiliar city during a torrential downpour is always a unique experience. When the rain eventually subsided, I found Dunedin to be striking in comparison to many other Florida cities for its absence of commercial signs and corporate franchise restaurants. Dunedin also lays claim to being the place where frozen orange juice concentrate originated. [28]

Before departing Dunedin, I received a message from the company's Safety Department indicating that I would be required to attend a defensive driver's class in Knoxville because of the incident in Jacksonville. This made my day! After that, I got another series of three eighty-eight mile runs between High Springs and Jacksonville—another Trifecta from Hell. This day just kept getting better!

Upon completion of my second *Trifecta*, I was seriously considering the merits of switching to the National fleet. It offered a three-cent per mile pay increase along with more miles than I was getting on this Coke fleet. It also came with the added bonus of no longer working with Dispatcher Bob. He and I had never been on the same page in regard to our working relationship, and it was growing tiresome to constantly argue with him. I was not the only one who was having problems with Dispatcher Bob. Tony indicated that he was also considering changing fleets. The National fleet was unquestionably starting to gain appeal.

We set out for Clinton, Tennessee after the Trifecta. Clinton's original name was Burrville in honor of Aaron Burr, the Vice-President under Thomas Jefferson. Burrville was renamed because of the disgrace of the Burr-Hamilton duel that resulted in the death of Alexander Hamilton.[29] The name Clinton was probably selected because George Clinton was one of Burr's political rivals. Along with Hamilton, George Clinton helped to destroy Burr's bid for the governorship of New York.[30]

Kitty and I spent the night in Clinton and prepared to pick up a load in Atlanta in the morning before going home for the weekend. Kitty now recognized the word "home." She meowed more furiously when I asked, "Do you want to go home?"

My decision to switch to the National fleet was not yet etched in granite, but the hammer and chisel were definitely in my sight.

Week 27: "Shagged" again!

We went all the way from Scottsboro to Orlando on Sunday night. That was not my original intention, but we left later than planned and it was the only option to make the delivery on time.

I got irritated when the security guard in Orlando told me I would have to wait a long time to be unloaded. My irritation, as it turned out, was unfounded as I was one of the first to receive a dock assignment. I'd had a lot of trouble with this dock last time but, this time, I nailed it on the first attempt. The Florida heat was relentless, so I was content to sit in my air-conditioned truck the entire time.

Afterward, we got another series of loads from High Springs to Jacksonville and back. I could not believe that Dispatcher Bob assigned me a third *Trifecta from Hell*. I cannot say for certain, but this might have been when I decided to switch to the National fleet. To make matters worse, a forklift driver in Jacksonville accused me of hitting the fence the last time I was there or as he referred to it, "*My* fence." I knew darned well that I had not hit the fence, so I asked him to show me the damage and let me speak to the person who allegedly saw me do it.

"My fence has already been fixed," he replied.

He conveniently dodged my second request but persisted with his accusation. In so many words, I conveyed to him that he either needed to make a formal complaint to my company or shut his damned mouth! Otherwise, I intended to complain to <u>his</u> supervisor. After an exchange of more choice words, I brushed him off with a hearty *harrumph* and returned to my truck. I never heard anything more about the matter.

We sat in Jacksonville all night because the customer refused delivery until the next morning, even though I arrived on time. Dispatcher Bob told me that I would receive thirteen and a half hours detention pay, but I never got it. After this third Trifecta; dealing with the ***my fence*** guy, and needlessly sitting idle, I made a firm decision to put in a request to switch to the National fleet.

Next morning, we picked up another load in High Springs and delivered to the Coke plant in Knoxville. I headed toward home after delivery, but Dispatcher Bob nailed me with a shag run from Knoxville to Vonore, Tennessee. In trucking vernacular, "shag" is not a pleasurable experience. It is a very short trip for which the company pays an additional stipend; an amount that is almost always too small to warrant the time, trouble, and aggravation of the shag. This one, however, went smoothly and I actually received my extra pay for this one…unlike the last time.

I was happy to get home after this troublesome week. I called Dick, my terminal manager, and formally requested to switch to the National fleet.

Week 28: Here Kitty, Kitty

We left on Monday because I had to go to the Defensive Driver's class in Knoxville due to my mishap in Jacksonville. This would set me up for a crappy paycheck this week.

I had a frightening moment on the way to Knoxville as I was pulling my empty trailer up a hill in the pouring rain. As I felt the trailer begin to fishtail, a leaden feeling emerged in the pit of my stomach. Thankfully, I managed to accelerate and stabilize it before it went out of control, but the terrifying experience caused my butt cheeks to clamp together so tight they could have bent a quarter. It drove home the point that it was more dangerous to pull an empty trailer than a loaded one—especially in the rain. An empty trailer is also more likely to be blown over in high winds. This is usually not a concern until a driver actually feels his truck violently rocking to and fro in the midst of gale force winds.

There was nowhere to park at the small Knoxville terminal, so I dropped my trailer at a nearby truck stop. I was lucky to find a spot as it was filling up rapidly when we arrived.

I left my truck in the terminal shop for service and repair while I was in class the following day. I hated to leave Kitty in the truck in her portable carry-kennel all day, but I had little choice.

There were many other drivers attending the DDC class. One driver was there because of failing to hook up to his trailer correctly and then driving out from beneath it. I am sure it was a lonely day in his mind when he heard the sickening thud. Everyone here shared at least one thing in common: we had all, in varying degrees of severity, screwed up. My faux pas, I would later learn, was comparatively minor to many.

DDC class was a snooze fest. They gave us our driving test in a mini-van, which I found to be laughable. On a positive note, they treated us to an excellent lunch at the Texas Roadhouse in

Knoxville. It wouldn't compensate for the inevitable crappy paycheck, but I appreciated getting a meal at a decent place.

When I got back from class, Kitty's kennel was not in the truck and she was nowhere to be found. I enlisted the help of a shop mechanic to determine her whereabouts. Someone had moved her kennel inside to the air-conditioned office area. Had I known this were an option, I would have pursued it myself. I was glad that someone took the initiative to move her inside, but a note would have spared me some undue stress. This would have prevented the necessity of a half-hour Kitty quest.

We finally got back on the road on Wednesday with a load going to the Coke plant with hellishly tight docks in Charlotte, North Carolina. After several attempts, I succeeded in contacting my terminal manager to confirm my request to switch to the National fleet. He was evasive at first, but I gained my confirmation after threatening to quit. It was official now; I would be going to the National fleet in one week.

I told Dispatcher Bob that I would run this weekend because of the two days I'd spent in DDC class. Therefore, after delivery in Charlotte, I expected to get a weekend run. Instead, Dispatcher Bob sent me a load that delivered to Jacksonville on Monday morning. Thinking there was no weekend freight available, I picked up the load in Atlanta and then headed toward home. Upon arriving in Scottsboro, the Qualcomm beeped. It was Dispatcher Bob with a belated query as to whether I wanted to drop this load in High Springs and then pick up another one. I told him I was already home, and I would deliver on Monday as per the load assignment. The Qualcomm then beeped with another message from Dispatcher Bob, but I ignored it. Then, I called Brian to tell him about the latest Dispatcher Bob-ism. Brian said that he would have told Dispatcher Bob, flat out, to kiss his ass.

Week 29: Goodbye Dispatcher Bob

We begrudgingly left on Sunday to go to Jacksonville. It is always hard to hit the road again after a brief time at home, but it's not so bad once we're out. Kitty and I spent the night at the Florida Welcome Center on I-75, and I rejoiced in the knowledge that this was my last week with Dispatcher Bob.

Next morning, we waited forever to be unloaded in Jacksonville. Dispatcher Bob had pre-planned me on a load to Boynton Beach, Florida, but it would have been a challenge even if we had been emptied immediately—and we weren't. Dispatcher Bob had a propensity for scheduling impossibly tight pre-plans. Then, he'd blame it on the driver when it didn't get there on time. This was among the many reasons I was leaving Dispatcher Bob's fleet.

I managed to dismiss myself from the Boynton Beach run when Dispatcher Bob reluctantly accepted the mathematical impossibility of it. We went to Bama Budweiser in Anniston, Alabama instead. We spent the night at a ridiculously packed TA in Baldwin, Florida. I had planned on getting a shower, but the mass of humanity inspired me to settle for a bird bath.

I weighed my beer load the next morning and then went across the road to the Pilot for fuel. The morning started on a sour note when I discovered that the left fuel pump was broken. I had to drive through the fuel island twice to fill both tanks. The clerk, at least, gave me a free cup of coffee for my trouble.

We made it to Tallapoosa, Georgia for the evening where I had dinner at the Huddle House next to the truck stop and struck up a conversation with a waitress. I am generally reserved around strangers but, after spending hours alone on the road, I sometimes surprise myself by getting chatty with anyone who will listen. Kitty is a good listener, but it is nice to occasionally talk to a being with a more sophisticated vocabulary than "Meow."

I quickly forgot the enjoyment of my meal and conversation as I walked across the truck stop parking lot afterward. Although I liked this Tallapoosa truck stop because of the ample parking space, the olfactory bouquet wafting across the lot on this night was akin to raw sewage. This theme tends to repeat itself consistently at this particular truck stop. I put Tiger Balm on my arches before bed, and its pungent odor helped to drown out the disgusting smell.

There was no one at the customer when we arrived in Anniston the next morning, and I fiercely needed to relieve myself. I did my best to wait until someone came, but circumstances forced me to find a wooded area and take care of business. Having toilet paper on board the truck is sometimes just as crucial as having fuel.

After Anniston, we picked up another load in Chattanooga to deliver, once again, to the horribly small-docked Coke plant in Charlotte. I called Dick to confirm that everything was set for me to switch to the National fleet on Monday.

Our final duty for the Coke fleet sent us to Newnan, Georgia. I cannot recall the name of the North Carolina town where we picked up the load, but it was in the midst of the Green River Gorge.

The remote Green River Gorge is a rugged landscape of steep ravines, coves, and a mixed hardwood forest that also offers an impressive array of whitewater rapids. At one point, the Green River drops four hundred feet in a distance of one and a half miles and runs through a six-foot wide crevice known as the Narrows. The 225-foot high bridge across the Gorge on I-26 is the highest in North Carolina, and one of the largest in the United States.[31]

I ran as hard as I could to get to Newnan before I was out of hours only to discover that the customer would not accept delivery until after midnight. I was tempted to go and try a club sandwich at Newnan's Redneck Corner Café while I waited. The Redneck Café makes claim to an array of hot sauces "so ferocious they come with an eyedropper."

I had one last fight with Dispatcher Bob, as he wanted to run me over the weekend instead of sending me home. I told him there were many reasons I needed to go home before switching to the National fleet, not the least of which was that I did not wish to start out with limited hours to work. After playing phone tag with Dick and Dispatcher Bob for about an hour, I finally got my way. I have found that keeping a level head and arguing with calm logic without lapsing into a "redneck rampage" frequently gets me what I'm asking for if it is within reason.

I called Brian from Newnan and told him that I was now making my last delivery for the Coke fleet. He was glad I was getting out from beneath the thumb of Dispatcher Bob. Tony had also made it official that he would be leaving the Coke fleet. Rumors were floating around that the arbitrary reign of Dispatcher Bob might be winding down to an end.

I was excited to be going to the National fleet but, despite everything, I was glad to have gotten some experience with the Coke fleet first.

Week 30: A Kansas Moon

I greeted my first day on the National fleet with enthusiasm. Unfortunately, I had to do two short shag runs between plants in Scottsboro before picking up my load in Florence, Alabama. This put me behind schedule right out of the starting gate. The first load delivered to Tiffin, Ohio the next day, so I was forced to run later than I prefer in order to make the delivery appointment. I ran until 10pm and spent the night at the Kentucky Welcome Center on I-65.

The next day was not fun. It rained all day, and a serious accident in Dayton promised to shut down the interstate for hours. Information from the CB radio said that a big truck was hanging from an overpass. In an effort to avoid this mess, I took an exit ramp in Dayton. I had no clue where I was going as I frantically tried to read my map on the move while praying for a lengthy red light. It came as no surprise to see a green light at every intersection. Fortunately, I guessed correctly and found my way out of Dayton to resume my rainy trek. Kitty and I made it to Tiffin with a whole five minutes to spare.

Author's Note: I cannot recall, exactly, when I began seeing Truck Driver GPS systems in truck stops but, in early 2006, very few trucks had a dashboard GPS to assist the driver. Abrupt changes in plans, like the one mentioned above, were usually a seat-of-the-pants operation if the territory was unfamiliar. Fortunately, very few trucks nowadays do NOT have dashboard GPS devices. While they aren't perfect, and they are no replacement for common sense, I can personally attest that they certainly help out in a pinch.

Tiffin is a small Ohio town with an interesting history. Located between Columbus and Toledo, Tiffin's St. Paul's Methodist Church was the first church in the world to be lit by Thomas Edison's light bulb.[32] When Edison heard about the progressive move of incorporating electrical service by the people of Tiffin, he presented the church with a beautiful brass chandelier, which still lights the church today.

An epiphanic light bulb, however, did not appear above my head as I approached the dock of my Tiffin customer. The dock lay at an awkward angle, and the rain had transformed the docking area into a swampy mire. There were no visible landmarks on the ground to use to align the trailer, and the relentless downpour exacerbated the situation further. I thought I would never get the truck to the dock straight, and I lost my cool in the form of a personal tirade after many failed attempts. After what seemed like an eternity, I finally docked at an acceptable angle.

"If it makes you feel any better," consoled the forklift driver, "I've seen guys who've been driving for twenty years have trouble with that dock."

I appreciated his attempt, but it actually didn't make me feel any better.

After the debacle at the customer, I was exhausted. I pulled into an empty supermarket parking lot to spend the night. Shortly after parking, another trucker pulled in to ask directions. Thanks to the recent addition of *Streets and Trips* software to my toolkit of the road, I was able to help him. Supplemental mapping software was a godsend. It was definitely cutting down on my helpless calls to customers and shippers after receiving faulty directions from the company.

I had intended to give my new travel stove a test run tonight, but I was too drained to mess with it. I settled for a cold sandwich and a warm, welcoming bed.

The next day went more smoothly even though it rained again for most of the day. Our next load was going to Sidney, Nebraska. The directions I received appeared more as if I'd be looking for "Hoot Owl Holler" in the Okefenokee Swamp. The Sidney customer was so far out in the sticks, even my supplemental software couldn't find it.

The next day was an uneventful driving day of 643 miles. While getting fuel in Aurora, Nebraska, a truck hauling livestock, or a "bull runner" pulled into the fuel island next to me. A gentle breeze wafted the odoriferous ensemble in my direction. In my Navy days, I smelled beer and pickled egg farts that were more palatable. There isn't enough gold in Ft. Knox to entice me to drive a bull runner.

The skies finally cleared and the rain subsided. We made it all the way to the Wal-Mart in Lexington, Nebraska. There were no parking spots when we arrived, but a truck pulled out just as I was about to pass behind him. I pointed to the sky and said, "I owe you one."

Kitty sensed that we were at a place that would provide her with a treat, so she became excited and vocal. She slept most of the time when the truck was moving, but sometimes, she grew tired of the endless miles and became inspired to perform a feline concert as we rolled down the road to voice her discontent. She was a vocal cat to begin with, and a *Meow medley* at an inopportune time often made me irritable as well. In spite of this, it was much better out here with her company. She was worth every bit of the trouble and extra work. On this evening, I treated her appeals with an all-you-can-eat portion of a roasted lemon chicken. After gorging herself, she climbed into the sleeper and curled up in a euphoric slumber.

We rolled into Sidney on Friday morning, and the directions were not as bad as I had feared. I had no trouble finding the place, but I almost got stuck in the mud while we were there. Thank goodness for the inter-axle differential switch in the cab. This causes both axles on the rear of the tractor to work in conjunction as drive axles.

Sidney, Nebraska owes its origins to the transcontinental railroad. Founded in 1867 by the Union Pacific, the town grew up around the military base of Fort Sidney, where soldiers guarded the railroad against Indian attacks.[33] Sidney prospered greatly when gold was discovered in the Black Hills in 1874. The community also served as the railhead for equipment and supplies moving north. Shortage of sleeping accommodations led to the establishment of the world's first all-night theater, and a front street lined with eighty saloons, gaming halls, brothels, and boarding houses. This earned Sidney the moniker of Sinful Sidney: The Toughest Town in the Western Frontier.[34]

While I was more of a mudslinger than a gunslinger in Sidney, I was happy to live to tell the tale. We picked up our next load in McCook, Nebraska, which was destined for Brownsville, Texas with a stop-off in Houston.

On the way to Texas, I encountered a Kodak moment on US23 just past Oberlin, Kansas. A row of at least a dozen cows stood side-by-side, pointing their hindquarters through the fence and toward the highway. They seemed to be issuing a collective "bovine moon" to all passersby. This provided a welcome laugh.

After spending the night in Wakeeney, I discovered that there is actually an Oz museum in Kansas. I would have given anything to click my heels together three times when I got wedged in behind a school bus at a truck stop in Oklahoma City. As I waited helplessly for the entire pubescent caravan to disembark, I watched most of the adolescent boys frantically pump their arms in an effort to coerce me into blowing the road horn. Engulfed by the wave of pre-teens, I merely shook my head and said, "This can't be happening."

We spent the night in Denton, Texas where a Lot Lizard knocked on my window as I was reading my USA Today. "Lot Lizard" is a term used to refer to truck stop prostitutes. The drug-induced haze of the lizard inspired a mixed feeling of disgust and pity. My lizard encounters have been infrequent; most truck stops have taken measures to eliminate the scourge. There are, however, still a few Texas truck stops with lizard infestations.

After an invitation for "commercial company," her pitiable and unkempt appearance elicited a simple and concise "no" from me. I then rolled up my window, knowing that nightmares probably waited in the sleeper berth.

Detour: Lot Lizards

Many consider lot lizards to be the lowest rung on the ladder of the oldest profession. The girls and women who shuttle between the shadows of trucks seeking money in exchange for sexual favors have long since abandoned any shred of self-respect. These women are often trying to support a drug habit, and there is little sympathy for what many consider the scourge of the trucking industry.

My first lizard encounter occurred when I was riding with Ringo. After purchasing a hot dog at a Florida truck stop, an old purple Plymouth Duster, that looked like it had collided with a telephone pole, blocked my path to Ringo's truck. Two scantily dressed women, appearing to be in their late twenties, occupied the decrepit vehicle. The blonde woman on the passenger's side beckoned me down to her level and inquired as to whether I would be interested in "commercial company".

I could tell that, at some point, this woman had been pretty. The bone structure of her face was angelic, but acne now peppered her features, and her eyes were glassy with a drug-induced haze. I thought my eyes were deceiving me when I actually thought I saw stretch marks on her cheeks.

My first thought was, "I wonder how that happened?"

Sadly, I thought I probably knew.

Who are the women willing to rent their bodies to strangers driving big rigs? According to an article by Max Heine, they range from teenage runaways to aging, battered spouses. Many turn tricks part time and, for others, it is a full-time job. Many are seeking drug money, and most show a frightening lack of concern for sexually transmitted diseases. Heine goes on to say that the one thing common to most of them is a tragic background of abuse.[35]

Despite their often worn down appearance, lot lizards retain their marketability because over-the-road trucking has a way of highlighting basic needs. Truckers are accustomed to pulling out their wallets for things taken for granted at home, such as a meal or a shower. Some truckers succumb to the loneliness of the road and are willing to pull out their wallet for company as well. I have personally talked to one trucker who claimed to have paid a Lot lizard twenty dollars just to sit in his truck and talk to him. He was not looking for sex—just company.

Most truckers, however, view Lot lizards with disgust and reproach. The few who are willing to pay the price for sex may, ultimately, pay a much higher price in the form of a sexually transmitted disease.

As one driver says, "To watch one girl get into twenty trucks in the course of one night is pretty damn frightening! What on earth are these guys thinking?"

Lizard infestation at truck stops has reduced dramatically in recent years. Many truck stops have taken a tough stance by hiring security, putting up fences, and increasing lighting. Most truck stop managers are quick to call law enforcement at the report of a lizard sighting. Truck stops care about their image, but the lizard scourge is still a problem in some areas.

Many drivers take personal measures to repel lizards. A "No Lot Lizards" sticker can be purchased in most major truck stops. Some drivers paint a woman's name on the door, and others display an "I Love My Wife" bumper sticker. A creative method employed by one driver showed a bra and a giant pair of panties hanging in plain view at the front of the cab. There are various lizard-repelling techniques, but none will deter the most determined from banging on the door in the middle of the night.

A more recent lizard encounter of mine occurred at a truck stop in Huntsville, Texas. I looked up from reading my USA

Today to see that I was too late to hide from an approaching lizard. The woman appeared to be in her forties or fifties, and her shorts were at least two sizes too small. Rolls of flesh on her upper body fought the good fight to escape the bonds of a stained halter-top. As she stepped up to my window, an insincere smile revealed a missing row of teeth, and the unmistakable smell of alcohol and tobacco assaulted my senses.

"My name is Merle," she crooned. "Are 'ya lookin' for some company?"

It was with a mixture of disgust and pity in observing this particular Merle was downright haggard. (No disrespect intended toward the country music legend.)

Though I cannot help feeling a degree of sympathy for a lizard, it has a strict boundary. I am more inclined to give a twenty dollar tip to a hardworking waitress than to a skanky Lot lizard with no regard for her own (or anyone else's) health and well-being.

Week 31: A Loose Nut in Texas

Sunday was a short day as we drove just over two hundred miles to Huntsville, Texas. The brutal Texas heat was like a sweltering fist that knocks you back when you open the door, and makes you whimper with its wrathful assault.

Huntsville is located in the East Texas Piney Woods on the I-45 corridor between Houston and Dallas. Huntsville became the home of Sam Houston, who served as President of the Republic of Texas. A 67-foot statue commemorates Houston's life in Huntsville and it is the world's largest statue of an American hero.[36] Travelers on I-45 are hard-pressed to miss it.

It was too hot to remain outdoors for long, so I stayed in the truck and played computer games for most of the day. We left on Monday morning for the stop-off delivery in Houston. It went well except for having trouble locating the customer—none of the buildings bore numbers. After the stop-off delivery, we were off to Brownsville, Texas.

Brownsville is the southernmost city in Texas lying on the U.S.-Mexico border. It is the largest city in the Rio Grande Valley, in both size and population. On December 25, 2004, Brownsville had its first measurable snowfall in 109 years. With one and a half inches of snow, Brownsville recorded its first-ever White Christmas. The snow was later sold on eBay.[37]

On the way to Brownsville, a four-wheeler passed me on US77 just south of Victoria, Texas. My attention immediately piqued as a fiery display of sparks spewed from beneath the boat trailer towed by the four-wheeler. I did a double-take before realizing that the boat trailer was missing a tire, and the driver appeared oblivious to the scorching trail he left behind. The driver of a container truck passed me a minute later, and I warned him about the four-wheeler on the CB. He said that he'd been behind this guy when the tire flew off. We talked for a few minutes in an attempt to discern what kind of drugs the four-wheeler might be abusing. How could he be oblivious to what was happening?

It took about twenty miles, but Sparky finally pulled to the shoulder. I felt sure that the boat trailer did not contain the only loose nut here.

Brownsville was not fun. The customer was on a dirt road! To make matters worse, my directions provided the incorrect name of the client. I passed it by at least three times as I drove in circles. If not for assistance from a local, I may never have found it. After finding it, I almost wished I hadn't. Docking required a blindside maneuver off the tiny dirt road. The heat was more brutal than ever, and I was a sweaty, dirty wreck by the time I finally docked.

After delivery, I parked on the side of the dirt road next to Rio Grande Tool Company, hoping I wouldn't get a ticket for spending the night there. Fortunately, no one bothered me.

We waited until 9am for dispatch to send us to Laredo the next day. I ran US83 parallel to the Rio Grande. I saw almost no truck stops along a desolate highway, so I was thankful that I had not filled my gigantic coffee mug this morning.

I would not have thought it possible, but Laredo seemed even hotter. Laredo's positioning between Mexican mountains to the west and the Gulf of Mexico to the east is responsible for its sweltering weather. The deserts of Northern Mexico also influence much of Laredo's hot and dry weather, and the mountain range cuts off the moisture from the ocean.

The searing heat was not the only challenge in Laredo. Dozens of trucks rumbled about the shipper's docking area in apparent disarray. The tempers of many drivers rose to the degree of the relentless summer heat as vehicles blocked and impeded one another's path. To make matters worse, few of the shipping personnel spoke adequate English. I combed my memory for a few Spanish phrases from my distant past, but all I could retrieve was, "¿Cómo estás?", "¿Dónde está el baño?", and "¡Feliz Navidad!"

When I finally received my dock assignment, I discovered that another driver had stolen it from me. Shipping then told me to take any available dock but, when I took one, they came out and asked me to move again. By the time I reached the grand finale of this three-ring circus, I'd had my fill of Laredo.

This load's destination was Denver. Mercifully, we got out of Laredo and found a little truck stop in Dilley, Texas to stay for the night. As I prepared to heat up some canned food for supper, I spied a Church's Chicken across the road—then, all bets were off! I filled up on Church's (after giving Kitty a generous share) and then went to bed with Kitty in a blissful slumber at my feet.

I drove all day on Wednesday after stopping in Big Spring, Texas to replace a headlight. I slept poorly because of suffering charley horses in the arches of my feet all night. This still sometimes happened after a long day of driving or after using the clutch a lot. The countless small Texas towns we had passed through today required plenty of stop-and-go driving. After my initial screams of agony from my feet contracting into talons, I got up three or four times to apply Tiger Balm to my arches. This provided temporary relief, but I had little success in going back to sleep before the next painful episode ensued.

I was tired and cranky as we left the next morning, and the experience in Denver would do nothing to improve my attitude. I had to back into the dock off Denver's busy Brighton Boulevard while traffic impatiently waited on me. It became even more nerve-wracking as some of the vehicles refused to wait. While backing into the dock, I also had to ensure that I wasn't about to run over an impatient four-wheeler. The customer provided no traffic control; they just left me to my own devices.

I was so rattled by the time I got into the dock that I called dispatch and told them I would refuse to deliver there again without traffic control. The blame for an accident, in all likelihood, would fall squarely on the shoulders of the truck driver. I went to the Pilot in Denver after delivery and had yet another argument with dispatch. They wanted me to pick up another load today despite my lack of hours. I was completely drained and had nothing left to offer on this day. We spent the night in Denver.

We received a load assignment on Friday morning from the Purina plant in Denver to Tampa, Florida. I went to Purina and learned that the freight would not be ready until the next morning. For that reason, we went back to the Pilot and spent the rest of the day watching movies.

I returned to Purina Saturday morning to find out the load still wasn't ready. I wanted the Tampa run, but this was getting silly. I called dispatch to see if they could take me off this assignment and put me on one that actually existed. They found a Budweiser load from Fort Collins, Colorado to Columbus, Mississippi. This wasn't as good as the Tampa run—it was akin to having a T-bone under your nose and suddenly having it snatched away and replaced with pimento loaf. However, the Tampa run wasn't of much use if I could not get the freight. I was content to set out for the Anheuser-Busch plant in Fort Collins.

Fort Collins enjoys a thriving beer culture. There are three microbreweries in the city, which include the New Belgium Brewing Company, the Odell Brewing Company, and the Fort Collins Brewery. Fort Collins also plays host to the annual Colorado Brewer's Festival.

After arriving in Fort Collins, the security guard could not find my pickup number for the load.

Here we go again!

I had to park and wait for about an hour while the dispatcher carefully extracted his head from his rectum. Upon successful extraction, he gave me another load offering. I had a choice between San Diego, Los Angeles, or El Paso, Texas. I did not relish the idea of returning to the Texas heat, but I wanted to go home next week, so I took El Paso.

We got our load of beer and headed back toward Denver. We passed by John Elway's Chevrolet dealership, and I was hoping to get a glimpse of John selling a car. To my disappointment, he wasn't there.

We spent the night at the Tomahawk truck stop in Fountain, Colorado where I had dinner at a quaint little restaurant called Biscuits Café. The service was friendly and the atmosphere was soothing, both in stark contrast to all of the earlier events of the week. Unfortunately, next week was destined to see little improvement.

Week 32: El Paso, Pecos, and a Cracked Radiator

After a long driving day, I was unable to locate the TA in Albuquerque, New Mexico where I was supposed to get fuel. This truck stop is off the beaten path and many drivers have trouble finding it if they've never been there before. The company provided a "fuel solution" in an effort to minimize fuel costs. After a call to dispatch, they allowed me to fuel in Lemitar, New Mexico instead.

We encountered one of the more uniquely named cities when we drove through Truth or Consequences, New Mexico. Formerly called Hot Springs, the city took the name of a popular radio program in 1950 when *Truth or Consequences* host Ralph Edwards promised to do the program from the first town that named itself after the show.[38] Truth or Consequences is renowned for its year-round beautiful climate and is a popular retirement community. It was also the fictional hometown of Cactus Jack, one of the professional wrestling personas of Mick Foley.

We wrapped up the day at a truck stop in Vado, New Mexico, which was only about an hour from our destination in El Paso. The truck stop suffered an unbelievable fly infestation; they blanketed the windshield and the outside of the vehicle to the point where it became unsettling. It deterred me from going inside the facility until they slowly began to thin out. Cow pastures encompassed the area around the two truck stops there, which helped to explain the abundance of flies.

We arrived at the El Paso Budweiser plant on Monday morning only to endure a five-hour wait. A Mexican woman made entrepreneurial rounds to the waiting drivers in an attempt to sell homemade burritos. Her endearing personality inspired me to buy one. Nonetheless, as I bit into it, I fervently hoped that the meat had originated from a bovine source. It tasted fine though, and it passed Kitty's taste test with flying colors as well.

After a long wait, we made the delivery and picked up our next load at another business in El Paso. As I searched for the place, I accidentally turned into the airport exit. This forced me to make a tight U-turn and go the wrong way on a one-way street to get out. This was the second time I'd made an unscheduled tour of an airport, and I hoped it would be the last.

This load would go to Forest Park, Georgia in the Atlanta suburbs, and then we'd head home. I had just enough time to make it to the Flying J in Pecos, Texas for the night. Pecos is located about two hundred miles east of El Paso, and its local cultivation of cantaloupes has earned widespread recognition. Pecos also claims to be the site of the world's first rodeo in 1883.[39]

On Tuesday, I hoped to make it to the Pilot in Haughton, Louisiana, but I got a *Low Coolant Level* alarm on I-20 in Texas causing my truck to shut down twice. If the coolant drops below a certain level, a sensor causes the engine to shut down. I added two jugs of water, and that bought me enough time to get to Love's just across the Louisiana state line in Greenwood. I then called the shop at my home terminal and they told me to buy more coolant and "keep an eye on it."

Thanks a lot! I would have done that anyway.

Now, I knew I'd be paranoid about this all day tomorrow.

The next day, I planned to go to Tallapoosa, Georgia but when I stopped at a rest area in Eutaw, Alabama, I saw that my paranoia was not unfounded. The coolant leak had worsened. After calling the company's breakdown hotline, they sent me to the TA in Cottondale, Alabama. The mechanic at TA told me that my radiator was cracked—there was nothing he could do. Now, I'd have to take my truck to the Freightliner dealership in Birmingham in the morning. This made it impossible for me to make my delivery, so the next joy awaiting was to arrange for another driver to come get the load. Today had been a nightmare, and tomorrow didn't hold much promise of improvement.

We arrived in Birmingham on Thursday morning and, since the truck would not be ready until the next day, we spent the night in a motel. After the past couple of days, I felt I'd earned myself a couple of drinks from the bar next door to the motel.

On Friday, I waited a couple more hours at Freightliner before my truck was ready, but I finally got it back. The heavens opened up for a violent downpour just before I arrived in Scottsboro, and the driver's side windshield wiper flew away into oblivion.

This was perfect!

I got out in the rain and tied a doo-rag to the stump of the broken wiper to prevent it from scratching the windshield.

Home had never looked as inviting when I rolled into the Scottsboro truck stop on US72. I was happy to have lived through this harrowing week. I could not have known that the most harrowing week of my trucking career lay just ahead.

Week 33: The Nudist Camp and a Chicago Scrape

I called Dick, my terminal manager, on Monday with a request to come to Marietta for repairs. My truck was missing a windshield wiper, a crack had developed on the driver's windshield, and the engine was making an intermittent noise that sounded like a playing card flapping against bicycle tire spokes. Despite this, I still had to argue relentlessly to gain authorization to come to Marietta. "Deadheading," or running empty, meant that the company was not making money. Moreover, living one hundred and sixty miles from my home terminal often made it a challenge to keep my truck serviced on schedule. I hated to begin the week by arguing with Dick, but I wasn't about to take a load with my truck in its present condition.

We spent the night at the Marietta shop after the mechanic had said there were a couple more things to do in the morning. "It shouldn't take long," he promised.

I prepared myself for a long wait.

I got my truck back after lunch next day with a new windshield, new wipers, and a normal-sounding engine. We picked up our first load in Columbus, Georgia, which delivered to Minooka, Illinois.

I ran until 10pm and parked at a rest area in Gordon County, Georgia for the night. I hate driving at night because finding a place to park after the sun goes down becomes increasingly challenging. Tonight, we got lucky.

I prepared for a long driving day as I rolled out into the morning fog on Thursday. I passed a billboard on I-65 in Kentucky reminding me, "Hell is real." I could not have known this would prove to be prophetic later in the week.

We spent the night at a rest area in Wolcott, Indiana and arrived in Minooka on Friday morning. On the way to Minooka, I recalled the first time passing through Rose Lawn, Indiana with Merlin. It brought a smile to my face remembering when Merlin explained that the sign for the Sun Aura Resort in Rose Lawn is the gateway to a nudist community.

The Sun Aura has been around since the 1930's and it is the oldest nudist camp in the United States. There are over two hundred permanent campsites in the three hundred acre wooded area, and many of the sites have taken on a theme of their own. One might encounter sites such as Bald Beaver Drive, Kinky Corner, Old Goat Road, or the Muff-Inn.

A popular tourist attraction at the Sun Aura is a giant *Lady's Leg Sundial*. The lady's leg is sixty-three feet long and correctly positioned to tell time. The man who paints it says that a tourist need not get nude to take a picture of the giant leg. For those who do choose to get into the spirit of things, however, the Sun Aura offers a helpful sign on the exit road that reads: *Stop. You must be dressed beyond this point.*[40]

The delivery to Minooka went fine, and then I went to a nearby truck stop to await the next load assignment. Today was going well, but that ended when the Qualcomm beeped. The next pickup sent us into the heart of Chicago. Many drivers dread Chicago because of the many one-way streets, low bridges, endless construction, and insane traffic. Like New Jersey, Chicago is a terrible place for a new driver to get sidetracked.

Although the traffic was painfully slow, I found my Chicago shipper with little trouble. I had trouble getting into the garage-like dock because I couldn't see where I was backing with the sun glaring in my face. Some of the drivers seemed to have no problem with it, but the total absence of vision still posed a unique challenge for me.

After loading, I figured on going out the same way I'd come in. I certainly didn't want to get my directions fouled up in this city. I had passed beneath a low viaduct to get into the shipper, and I would pass beneath the other side of it to get out. As I approached it, I noticed that it looked very low, so I checked for height postings—I didn't see any. After passing beneath it on the opposite side, it never quite registered that it might be lower on one side than on the other.

My failure to consider this possibility became apparent when I heard a sickening scraping sound on top of the truck, and felt the mass of the vehicle shift downward. The shock and horror of this realization carried me to the midpoint of the bridge before I fully comprehended that the trailer was scraping the bottom of the viaduct. I was already halfway through, and there was traffic behind me, so I scraped the rest of the way out.

It felt as if an army of little men were inside me, shooting paintballs against the lining of my stomach. I could not stop in the middle of Chicago without causing a traffic jam. I had no choice but to keep going until I found a sensible place to stop.

After what seemed like an eternity, I made it to a service plaza and grudgingly climbed atop the spare tire on the back of the cab to assess the damage. Amazingly, there was no damage to the truck. The top of the cab condo sits slightly lower than the trailer, and it miraculously escaped the viaduct without a scratch.

The trailer was a different story.

The ribs on top of the trailer were bent as far as I could see while a three-foot gash assaulted the right seam. My heart sank, and the army of paintball men in my stomach recruited a new platoon. Not only would I have to call the dreaded Accident Hotline again, I was fearful that I might be fired over this.

After enduring a line of Gestapo-like questioning from the Accident Department, they told me to go to the TA in Gary, Indiana for repairs. The technician at TA sadly revealed that the trailer had structural damage and he did not have the means to fix it. After another series of sickening conversations with various company departments, I was told to go to the terminal in Lafayette, Indiana. By this time, I was out of hours and resolve, so I told them I'd have to go in the morning. Fortunately, it was not raining tonight. I was carrying a load of box fans wrapped in plastic, but I imagined the customer would still frown at having them rained on.

It came as no surprise when I slept poorly. Dealing with Chicago would have been bad enough, but with a disaster thrown in as a bonus topping, thoughts of quitting began to emerge again… if I wasn't fired first.

When I arrived in Lafayette the next morning, the shop technician heaved a weary sigh. His aspirations of a lazy Saturday at the shop just went swirling down the crapper. This promised to be an all-day job, and it would be well into the evening before the repairs were complete. I settled into the truck for a long day of watching movies and waiting.

In spite of the prospect of working in the sun perched atop a ladder all day, the shop technician, Kent, was a very affable fellow. His shoulder-length brown hair was tied in a ponytail to reveal a thick mustache that almost covered his mouth. Rippling, wiry muscles complemented his thin frame as he toiled in the sun all day. I stepped out to talk to him occasionally, and he welcomed the conversation. He introduced me to a little pub across the street called the Tick Tock. He suggested it as a good place for lunch.

The Tick Tock turned out to be a newfound gem. Along with a friendly, down-home atmosphere, I enjoyed some of the best pub grub I've had in quite some time. I hoped this would not be my last visit to the Tick Tock.

It was 5pm before repairs were complete, so I decided to stay at the terminal overnight and get an early start. I thanked Kent for his hard work, and then kicked myself for not offering to buy his lunch when I'd gone to the Tick Tock.

My spirits were still down over this whole debacle, and I was unsure as to what results would spring from it. However, I knew I needed to put it behind me and get my head in the game for the coming days. It would be tough—letting go of baggage is not atop my list of mastered skills.

Week 34: I Ain't Got No Quarters!

We left at 3am as planned, and I resolved to do my best to put the Chicago disaster behind me and regain a positive outlook. I called Brian the previous night to tell him what happened and to voice my concern over the possibility of being fired.

"No, they won't fire you," he assured me. "You'll lose some safety points and you'll probably have to go to DDC class again, but they won't fire you."

Brian's assurances made me feel better, but it would still be a while before I regained the ability to pass beneath a bridge without cringing.

This load was finally on its way to Prince George, Virginia, and we made it to the Pilot in Hagerstown, Maryland for the night. Despite my efforts to put the Chicago disaster behind me, I still slept badly.

We arrived at the Ace distribution center in Prince George the next morning only to discover that the appointment time was changed to the next day. I called dispatch and, after waiting an hour and a half, they authorized me to do a "drop and hook" at the customer. After dropping the loaded trailer and picking up an empty one, I awaited the next load offering.

After another hour of waiting, I attempted to call dispatch to see if there was a problem. They refused to answer the phone or respond to Qualcomm messages. I finally called the main office in Lincoln and asked to speak to someone who could tell me why dispatch was not responding. The receptionist transferred me to another line, but didn't tell me to whom I was being transferred.

"Yes," answered a gruff voice on the other end of the line.

I identified myself and expressed my concern over the dispatchers' refusal to respond to me in four hours.

"They're probably busy," he huffed.

"I can appreciate that," I replied, "but they don't appear to be busy getting me going so I can make money for the company."

He remained irritable throughout the conversation but, within five minutes thereafter, I had a load offering.

My curiosity was piqued since I never discerned whom I'd been speaking with in Lincoln. I called the receptionist back and asked her to whom she had transferred my call.

"I transferred you to *Mr. Kahuna's* office," she replied matter-of-factly.

Great! I thought. *Mr. Kahuna* was the company President. Not only had I recently suffered the Chicago disaster, I had now succeeded in aggravating the company President. Nonetheless, it had resolved my problem. We headed to South Boston, Virginia to pick up our next load, and I parked at a truck stop right across from the shipper for the night.

My fast food Achilles' heel had always been Bojangle's chicken, and this South Boston truck stop had a Bojangles restaurant with the best I'd ever tasted. I was in an upbeat mood after the outstanding chicken, but it was extremely short-lived.

I approached the clerk at the truck stop to get change for a dollar in order to get my daily dose of USA Today. The clerk looked as if she might have jumped right off the screen from the movie *Deliverance*, but I soon discovered that she was much more vocal than the film's banjo-picking star.

"I ain't got no quarters!"

She spat the double negative at me as if it were a plug of Levi Garrett.

"You gotta use th' change machine back 'round in th' cone-ur."

Her drawl wafted over an open cash register, and I peered in to see a change drawer brimming with quarters.

"Is it really too much trouble to give me four quarters?" I asked. "Looks like you've got plenty there."

"Yeah!" she spat back. "Use th' change machine!"

"Are you the manager?" I asked.

"No," she replied.

"I'd like to speak to the manager," I added.

Normally, I would not have had a problem with getting change from a change machine, even though it was on the opposite side of the truck stop. I had an issue with the attitude and indignation toward a paying customer.

When the manager walked out of his office, I knew that I'd made a mistake. If the clerk was the banjo picker from *Deliverance*, this was the guy who'd made Ned Beatty squeal like a pig. He had the same vacant, indignant look as the clerk.

"They ain't s'possed to give change out th' caish register," he drawled in a similar timbre. "She's jest doin' her job."

"Well," I replied, "if being rude to customers is her job, she's doing a fine one!"

His confused silence suggested that I might have bombarded him with an excessive number of syllables.

"Fine," I relented, "I'll use the change machine."

I half-expected to hear *Dueling Banjos* emerge as background music as I walked away.

I made the trek to the change machine only to see the *Out of Change* light brightly illuminated. I returned to the clerk to inform her that the beloved change machine was empty.

"Now, can I get change for a dollar?" I asked.

She grudgingly dug into the register and handed me four quarters with a snarl. By this time, I was beyond irritated, so I just tossed the dollar bill at her.

"Ya didn't have'ta 'thow' it at me!" she exclaimed.

"And you didn't have to be rude and run me in circles for four stinking quarters!" I shot back. I then paid her the tribute of a one-fingered salute as I left the store. It probably wasn't the right thing to do...but it felt like the thing to do at the time.

We left at 3am the next morning for our next destination—Findlay, Ohio. My fortunes did not seem to be improving as I went through Hillsville, Virginia in the Blue Ridge Mountains on US58. The sign for Lover's Leap should have provided a clue as to what lay ahead. Although the view of the area was spectacular with beautiful rock and wildflowers as a backdrop, the precipitous hills and winding roads did not allow the luxury of enjoying it for long. I was forced to crawl over Lover's Leap in sixth gear. Despite the slow going, the delivery to Findlay went fine, and we spent the night in the parking lot of the Wal-Mart distribution center there.

Findlay is home to Mark Metcalf, the actor who portrayed the anal-retentive Niedermeyer in the classic film *Animal House*. Findlay also had the distinction of being the only community in the world where touch-tone telephone service was available in the early 1960's.[41]

Driving across the mountains of Virginia had taken its toll on me, and I finally enjoyed a restful night's sleep. Kitty seemed tuckered out as well. When I had a rough day, she showed signs of stress from it too.

Our next delivery was from Perrysburg, Ohio to Vonore, Tennessee. It was already dark after delivering in Vonore, but I luckily found a parking spot at a small truck stop there. Shortly after parking, a huge thunderstorm arose with high winds that shook the truck violently. Storms rarely frighten Kitty, but she snuggled up next to me during this one. Oddly enough, the beating of the rain, the resounding claps of thunder, and the rocking of the truck had a calming effect on me, and I slept well.

Next morning, I discovered that the windshield, which was replaced in Marietta, was leaking. The maps and truck stop guides on the dash were soaked.

What a great way to start the day!

After cursing the Marietta shop under my breath, I set out for Newport, Tennessee to pick up the next load.

Newport is located in Cocke County and, from the 1920's through the 1960's, it became notorious throughout the southeast as a moonshine Mecca. At the onset of Prohibition in 1920, Cocke County was primed to meet the demand for illegally distilled liquor. Not only were there moonshiners with generations of experience, but the remote Appalachian hollows and thick forest provided perfect hiding places for illegal stills.[42]

I almost enjoyed an extended stay in Newport by getting stuck in a mud hole at the shipper. Fortunately, I managed to escape the mire and get on the way to North Platte, Nebraska. We spent the night about an hour east of Nashville after a relatively smooth and painless day.

I drove 615 miles on Saturday and made it to the terminal in Kansas City. More rain confirmed that my windshield was still leaking. I was in a bad mood by the time we got to Kansas City, and it did not improve when I spilled chili on my bunk while cooking dinner. The evening gained a perfect garnish when Kitty threw up in my seat. I instinctively thought of Al Bundy on *Married with Children* when he looks skyward and pleads, "Oh God! Is this all there is?"

Week 35: Eat More Possum

The Great Platte River Road Archway Monument on I-80 in Nebraska always captures my attention and awe as I pass beneath it. A 1500-ton structure that crosses over three hundred feet of a heavily traveled interstate, the Archway is a history museum that documents over a century and a half of transportation and communication across America. The Archway is also an interactive adventure that pays tribute to the pioneers who passed through Nebraska on their westward trip.[43] The exterior resembles a Nebraska sunset for passing motorists.

We made it to the Flying J in North Platte on Sunday, which is next door to the Wal-Mart distribution center where we deliver on Monday. It is often difficult to park at this busy truck stop, and today was no exception.

I went to the Wal-Mart D.C. a half hour before my appointment on Monday only for the guard to tell me to go out and come in again—I was in the wrong lane. I planned to turn around at the Flying J and come back, but I missed the driveway and had to go ten miles on the interstate before there was an exit on which to turn back. This day was not starting well.

It would not get better. We waited all day to be unloaded. I returned to Flying J afterward and requested dispatch to give me a pickup for tomorrow morning. It was already too late to get another load today. We got a run to Hermiston, Oregon—the site of my first solo delivery for this company.

We left on Tuesday morning for Aurora, Nebraska to pick up the Hermiston load. In 2003, the largest hailstone ever measured fell in Aurora. It had a diameter of seven inches and a circumference of 18.75 inches.[44] We were in the midst of a thunderstorm as we approached Aurora, and I hoped the record would not be broken today.

I saw a rolled-over tanker on the east side of Ogallala, Nebraska. The sight of a rollover always inspires shock and awe. I cannot help but think: *There, but for the grace of God, go I.*

We spent the night at the terminal in Cheyenne, Wyoming. The beauty of this part of the country still astounds me. The Rocky Mountains rise to snow-capped peaks and, below the timberline, evergreen forests of spruce, fir, and pine fill out the slopes. Most of the cities of the American west are small, and the spaces between them are significant. The large areas just seem to make it a little easier to breathe, and slightly more peaceful to be alive.

Wednesday was a long day of driving that ended in the Snake River Plain of Idaho. The Snake River Plain is a broad, bow-shaped depression that stretches for about four hundred miles and covers about a quarter of Idaho. Many of Idaho's major cities are in the Snake River Plain along with much of its agricultural land. The Snake River Canyon is in the Magic Valley region of southern Idaho. It remains well known as the site of an unsuccessful attempt to jump it by Evel Knievel in 1974. I can recall watching the abortive attempt on TV as a boy.

In a contraption called the Skycycle X-2, Knievel launched himself into celebrity history.[45] The Skycycle was comprised of a bucket seat attached to a steam-powered thrust engine designed to carry Knievel one mile across the canyon. It was then supposed to deploy a parachute and land on a pogo stick attached to its nose.

What could possibly go wrong?

The parachute accidentally deployed after launch, and Knievel crashed into the canyon below. Miraculously, he walked away with only minor injuries.

I was not at all tired after a long day of driving. I seem to have developed the necessary road toughness that I lacked in the beginning. Typically, it isn't my resolve that is the first to weaken—it's my bladder. Without mentioning names, I've known drivers who choose to use a jug while driving to avoid stopping. I elect not to. It not only poses a potentially dangerous distraction, but the threat of spillage is a convincing deterrent to me.

We passed a sign on I-84 in Oregon that read, *Eat/Gas*. I remain confused as to whether it suggests the consumption of petroleum or if it describes the succession of events that transpire by dining at the establishment.

We made it to Hermiston on Thursday and, astonishingly, got a parking spot at the crowded Pilot there. The delivery to Wal-Mart went fine on Friday morning but, after dropping my loaded trailer, I picked up an empty one that was a total piece of cow plop. I could have taken one that was slightly newer, but it sat securely in the center of an enormous mud puddle that seemed more pond than puddle. Next, we picked up a load of Starbucks coffee in Renton, Washington that delivered to Houston. I hoped to go home shortly after that run, so I was glad to be going in the right direction.

Another bird made a kamikaze run into my windshield on Saturday morning. My truck, apparently, presented an inviting image to our feathered friends as it rolled along the interstate—until the moment of impact, anyway.

We made it to a rest area just outside of Ogden, Utah for the night. When I got out, I noticed that someone had written a slogan in the dirt encrusted on the back of my trailer. I was left to wonder how long I'd been a rolling billboard, inviting the citizens of Utah to: *Eat more Possum.*

Week 36: Is that alligator staring at me?

On Sunday, we made it to Limon, Colorado, about an hour east of Denver. I spotted a bar across from the truck stop and, since I had not indulged myself in a drink in almost a month, I decided to go have a couple. Unfortunately, I ended up having more than a couple. There were plenty of other truckers in the bar, and listening to some of the stories from the old vets reminded me of what a rookie I still am.

Suffice it to say that Monday was a long day. I made the obligatory vow that I would never do that again while I'm on the road and, to this point, I haven't. After an endless day of pain and regret, I stopped near Wichita, Kansas for the night.

I had just enough time to get to the terminal in Wilmer, Texas on Tuesday. We got some rain in Oklahoma and my windshield continued its leaking ways. I decided to have my trailer inspected in Wilmer, and it's a good thing I did. One of the trailer dollies was damaged. I had no idea how it happened, but it was such that I had to get it repaired. Unfortunately, this eliminated my opportunity for a good night's sleep. Tomorrow would be my birthday, and I'd be content with the gift of a smooth, quick delivery followed by a load that sent me home.

After about three hours of sleep, we left for Houston at midnight. For a solo driver, the road provides many opportunities for thought and reflection. As I drove through Texas in the wee hours of the morning, I recalled marching in the Battle of Flowers parade in San Antonio during my marching band days at Haughton High School. The Battle of Flowers is an annual celebration honoring those who fought in the battles of the Alamo and San Jacinto. My days of deftly twirling drumsticks as I proudly marched with my snare drum are some of my fondest memories of youth. The Battle of Flowers parade, in 1977, served as the setting for a fourteen-year-old freshman to get his first kiss from LeAnn Bickley. I suppose everyone remembers their first kiss, and the magic of the first experience is rarely duplicated. I smiled at the sweet memory as I drove through the calm Texas night, and I politely mourned the loss of youth's innocence and magic.

After delivery in Houston, I began to feel the effects of only three hours of sleep. I decided to go to the Flying J in Houston and take it easy for the rest of the day. I went across the street to the Movie Tavern, a place where a server brings food and/or drinks while you enjoy the movie. I passed on the drinks, but the food was delicious. What a great idea this place was!

We went to the Budweiser plant in Houston on Thursday for our next load. The Shipping Department called the drivers on the CB radio for docking assignments but, unfortunately, my CB blew a fuse as I was waiting. I had to sit in the shipper's lobby for over three hours to receive my docking assignment. Dealing with a female security guard who carried a poisonous attitude around like a bag of snakes rendered my wait even less pleasant.

I hate picking up heavy loads, like beer or pet food, because the shipper almost never balances the weight correctly. If the weight exceeds 34,000 pounds on the front or rear trailer tandems, the adjustable tandems must be moved to balance the weight to legal standards. On a newer trailer this, usually, does not pose a problem but, on an older one, the locking pins are often rusted. This can require an extraordinary effort unless the aid of another driver is available. Needless to say, my tandems were impossibly stuck, and the delay only raised the ire of a security guard who was already as grumpy as a constipated goose.

It was getting late by the time I got out of the Budweiser plant, so I called it a day at a small truck stop in Winnie, Texas. I went to a Cajun restaurant called Al T's for dinner. The large main dining room was filled with dark wooden tables and chairs, and the walls were covered with fishing and hunting memorabilia. I could not avoid feeling a bit uneasy as mounted deer heads, fish, alligators, and sea turtles peered down at me with a lifeless stare. In addition to the standard Cajun fare of dirty rice, gumbo, and jambalaya, Al T's is also happy to serve up an alligator dish.

We left early the next morning for Natchez, Mississippi. The Budweiser warehouse in Natchez had a terribly tight dock in which I had to back from a narrow street. As I struggled with it, an impatient four-wheeler honked at me and I reflexively gave him the finger before I could filter my actions. I guess the nature of his business was, in his mind, far more important than mine.

After Natchez, we picked up the next load in Monticello, Mississippi that delivered to Cleveland, Tennessee on Monday. I planned to route myself through Scottsboro and spend the weekend at home. After delivering on Monday, I'd go back home for another three days. This was perfect!

Home was always a welcome sight, but the ritual of dropping the trailer at a truck stop, putting on the trailer door and kingpin locks, and unloading my belongings from the cab seemed to take forever. I planned to enjoy a weekend at home before delivering in Cleveland on Monday.

Detour: Spirituality on the Road

During the years I worked in the television business, I considered myself an agnostic. I did not reject the notion of God outright, but I was not convinced of His/Its existence either. Whatever the case, it didn't seem to make much difference in my life. Although I was a self-proclaimed agnostic, I still prayed from time to time. I figured that, at best, I was talking to God—at worst, it was a personal catharsis. It seemed like a win-win situation. In doing this, I suppose that I had, in some way, avoided uprooting the seeds of spirituality.

My experience in Cross Timbers, Missouri with Merlin and his family, and the people of that small community may have been the first event to pour some water upon those seeds. The camaraderie, love, trust, and pure selflessness I experienced there certainly rose above the human behavior to which I had been previously exposed. I could not help having a distinct "feeling" that something else was at play.

In the days to come, I would view the majestic beauty of a Wyoming sunrise, the rolling green hills of southern California, and the jaw-dropping craggy peaks of the Colorado Rockies. The sharply eroded pinnacles and spires in South Dakota's Badlands stretched for miles with no signs of civilization. It was difficult to observe natural beauty like that without getting a sense of wonder and awe and without getting a profound spiritual feeling—an instinct of something greater than myself that transcends human knowledge.

I have no doubt that my time on the road has afforded me the opportunity to explore the spiritual side of myself. The solitude of the road offers nothing if not plenty of time for thinking and personal reflection. I've pondered the big questions since I was a boy so, I immediately fell in love with philosophy after reading a book in the early 90's called *Sophie's World* by Jostein Gaardner. Finally, here was a mode of thinking that provided a different approach to the tough questions than the one offered by religion. Why are we here? Does God exist? Why is there evil in the world? Why can't people agree on what is moral? How should we live?

My mind was spinning with the new (to me) avenues from which to approach these questions. The great philosophers offered possibilities that did not seem like the unsatisfying cookie-cutter responses rendered by the church. It seemed like these guys had actually *thought* about it!

In saying this, I do not mean to disparage or promote anyone's belief system. I try to respect everyone's ideology whether I agree with it or not. This section is merely intended to illustrate the opportunity for introspective thinking afforded by driving on the interstate for ten hours a day. While some may choose to fill that void of solitude and silence with talk radio programs, music, or idle chatter on the CB radio, others reflect on the mysteries of life to become amateur road philosophers.

Okay, I get that you probably won't go up to an unshaven trucker with a stain of fifth-wheel grease streaked across his shirt at a truck stop and ask his opinion of existentialism or Nicomachean ethics. Frankly, I wouldn't blame you. You probably won't find many enthusiasts of propositional logic or metaphysics in a truck stop diner standing next to the rack of Stuckey's Pecan logs. I get it. And I'm certainly not claiming to be an expert on any of these topics. I'm just a guy for whom the road provided a sounding board for me to get inside my own head and clarify, redefine, or remain confused about some of life's questions. That's about it.

Unless you are one of those people who are "absolutely certain" of the truth of your philosophy or religion, or faith, or whatever…you also probably ponder the big questions from time to time. If you are one of those *absolutely certain* people, I say to you, "Congratulations!" As for the rest of us, we need to think about it.

Sure, a philosophy professor could probably punch my observations and musings full of holes without breaking a sweat but, at the end of the day, he'd be no closer to providing a concrete answer to the big questions than a trucker who is willing to think as he rolls along I-80 from Nebraska into Wyoming. But philosophy is really more about asking questions than getting answers. As a boy growing up in the rural South in the 60's and 70's, some questions were taboo. In a Southern Baptist Church of my youth, I certainly wouldn't have asked:

"Does God exist?"

Blue-haired old ladies would have fainted in shock, and pious deacons would have fished around in their Sunday vests for hidden flasks to calm their shaken resolve. There were certain questions that you just didn't ask. That's why discovering philosophy was such a breath of fresh air for me. Here was a brand of thinking that actually *encouraged* asking questions. This was my path, but I understand that it is not the path for everyone.

Indeed, I believe there are many paths toward spirituality, and that we each must find our own. Rolling down the road in an eighteen-wheeler helped to clear some of the brush from my particular path, but that was just me. The road is often lonely but, ironically, it is rarely boring. It has even provided some humor on the spiritual front. I recall a time when it seemed that someone (or something) attempted to guide me toward a particular spiritual path.

I had stopped at a rest area on I-20 in Norris, Mississippi and when I entered the men's room, I saw a series of pamphlets entitled *The Roman's Map to Heaven* strategically placed on top of the urinals. I thought that this would, perhaps, serve as a metaphor and, not unlike a pilgrimage to the Holy Land, I would be enlightened with an epiphany upon completing my quest and flushing. So, when I flushed, it was with great anticipation, but when the septic cycle had whirled to its conclusion, I remained standing in front of the latrine just as unenlightened as before. Despite my disappointment, I realized that I'd still had an epiphany of sorts. For I learned that if I were to ever, truly, discover a path to heaven, I probably wasn't going to find the directions perched atop a urinal in a Mississippi rest stop.

Even in choosing to explore a path of spirituality, I do not believe there is anything wrong with expressing doubt from time to time. Even my beloved Grandfather expressed religious doubt on occasion, though he was a devout Catholic. I considered this to provide more evidence that he was a thinking man rather than a bad Christian.

My Grandfather was, among other things, a talented carpenter who tinkered in various woodworking projects after he retired. I realized one day that he was doing basic algebra as he calculated an arc for a cabinet door that he was building. As a child and a young man during the Great Depression, he never went past eighth grade due to family responsibilities on the farm.

How is he doing algebra? I wondered. So, I asked him.

"Oh, I don't know," he humbly replied. "I just think on it till it starts to make some sense."

I hope to strengthen my own spirituality as the years pass, and I suppose that I'll just continue to "think on it till it starts to make some sense". In the meantime, I'll try and take in some aspects of life with wonder and awe, without requiring the empirical proof of a science experiment. Whether my faith is misplaced in doing so remains unanswered but, even if it ultimately proves wrong, isn't the risk of being wrong simply part of the experience of being human? I have to believe that's exactly what "God" would want me to do. At least, that's where I choose to put my faith as I roll down the highway.

Week 37 and 38: Kitty Foams at the Mouth

The delivery to Cleveland, Tennessee went fine on Monday and I was back in Scottsboro before noon for three more days off. As always, home time seemed to be over as soon as it started. I find it necessary to devote an entire day preparing to go back on the road. Between doing laundry, buying groceries and getting the truck cleaned and loaded for another stint out, the last day of home time is largely devoted to work.

We picked up our first load in Scottsboro on Friday slated for delivery to Niantic, Connecticut, a village in the town of East Lyme, Connecticut. We spent the night at the Petro in Knoxville. The first day on the road after home time often seems a bit surreal.

I got up at 3am and got a shower in the Petro, where I performed a "Ten-dollar Workout" with my resistance bands. I drove all the way to Shippensburg, Pennsylvania where we spent the night at Pharo's Truck Stop. I pondered as to why parking was so plentiful there until I heard the unmistakable sound of race cars zooming in close proximity. A stock car track lay beyond a hill across the road, and the cacophony of a competition was in full force. Fortunately, the melee subsided before bedtime.

On Sunday, I decided to take I-95 through New York City rather than going around on the bypass. Since it was Sunday, I hoped the traffic wouldn't be as bad. Some of the low bridges in the Bronx caused my sphincter to pucker, but we made it through the Big Apple without incident.

We spent the night at a service plaza near Madison, Connecticut. Kitty had begun sneezing before we left Scottsboro, and the episodes seemed to be worsening. On the advice of my veterinarian, I crushed up half a Benadryl tablet and sprinkled it on her food. After a couple of bites, Kitty sprang from her bowl as if a rattlesnake had leaped from it. She began moaning and hissing while foam flowed from her mouth. Clearly, Kitty did not like the taste of Benadryl. As a peace offering, I pinched up some of my smoked turkey for her after the poignant display. Her trust, however, was suspended, and it was almost two hours before she mustered the courage to eat it. On that night, Kitty slept in the front of the truck…I guess I can't blame her.

Located on Long Island Sound, Niantic Bay is popular for swimming, boating, and fishing. On Wednesday evenings and Sunday afternoons, the Niantic Bay Yacht Club organizes sailboat races, and multi-colored sails fill the Bay.[46]

There were no visible sailboats when we rolled into Niantic on Tuesday morning before the sun had risen. I assumed that we were delivering to a CVS distribution center, so I did a double take when I saw a small CVS pharmacy in a tiny plaza. Where was I going to put a 53-foot van at a small pharmacy?

No one was there when we arrived, so I parked alongside a bank to wait. When an employee arrived, he admitted that the 53-foot trailer was a surprise. Despite the logistical problems, we devised a plan and made the delivery. Afterward, we picked up our next load in Norwich, Connecticut.

Norwich is home to one of the most infamous figures of the American Revolution—Benedict Arnold. Kitty was slowly beginning to view me as less of a traitor because of the Benadryl episode, but she still cast a wary eye in my direction from time to time.

This load delivered to Ft. Wayne, Indiana with a stop-off in Baraboo, Wisconsin. I'd have to run like the wind to make both deliveries on time, so I resolved to drive as far as legally possible. It should not have surprised me when I accidentally pulled into the truck wash entrance at a Connecticut truck stop, and had to wait half an hour to get out. We made it to Carroll, Pennsylvania for the night, and Kitty's trust in me seemed finally restored.

The next day was a long day of driving that ended at the company terminal in Ottawa, Illinois. I had forgotten how small the terminal there was, and I was fortunate to get the last available parking space.

When returning to my truck after getting a shower in the terminal, a man in an RV pulled in with the desire to purchase fuel. He was utterly bewildered when I explained that he was in a private truck terminal. Despite the rumbling red Freightliners filling the yard, he remained unconvinced. Feeling no further obligation to provide additional evidence, I directed him to the nearest public fueling facility. He left—but he never managed to shed his mask of confusion.

I reluctantly arose at 1:45am to go to Baraboo, Wisconsin. Also known as Circus City, Baraboo is home to Circus World Museum, the former headquarters of the Ringling Brothers Circus.[47] It is now the largest library of circus information in the United States.

Aside from initially backing into the wrong dock, the Baraboo delivery went well. Afterward, I received a message from the company Safety Department to call them the next time I was at a terminal. I called them immediately to find out what it was about, but they refused to tell me until I was at a terminal. The cloak and dagger dialogue worried me. Was I in trouble? I did not need this black cloud hanging over my head.

The confusing request remained in the forefront of my mind after delivering to Ft. Wayne, Indiana. I called Brian and told him about the cryptic message from Safety.

"Piss test!" he immediately replied.

I heaved a sigh of relief, wishing I'd called him earlier.

The level of my worry suggested that the prospect of not being on the road upset me. Perhaps I liked being on the road… a little, at least.

We picked up the next load in Lima, Ohio, which delivered to Pineville, Louisiana. We spent the night just outside of Louisville, Kentucky.

Saturday was a long driving day that ended in Winona, Mississippi. Winona is known as "The Crossroads of North Mississippi" because of its central location at the intersection of Highways 51 and 82. The economy of Winona got a boost in May of 2005 with the addition of Pilot Travel Centers. The major truck stop chain purchased the High Point Truck and

Travel Center, previously owned by NFL player Kent Hull of the Buffalo Bills. The plaza opened completely in August of 2005, just a few days before Hurricane Katrina.[48]

The past two weeks had sailed along with relative ease, but the coming week would provide me with my most embarrassing moment as a truck driver.

Week 39: Roadside Emergency and a Walmart Bag

After delivering to Pineville, I got no subsequent load offering, so I parked on the side of the road next to the Procter & Gamble plant to spend the night. The truck leaned heavily to the starboard side, so I'm lucky that I sleep with my head on the port side. Sleep proved to be a challenge anyway. It was raining heavily and due to the starboard list of the truck, water leaked into the condo window and dripped onto my lower bunk. After enduring the Chinese water torture for a minute, I climbed up and stuffed paper towels into the leaking area. Unfortunately, that particular Band-Aid only helped for a little while.

I woke up at 7am after a restless night, and finally got a load offering from Lake Charles, Louisiana to Natrium, West Virginia. Natrium was not even on the map but, luckily, my Streets and Trips software found it. This was my first time hauling a hazardous materials load. The sodium hydroxide I picked up in Lake Charles was considered a corrosive. A hazardous materials load required special paperwork, a special license endorsement, and placards to be posted on all four sides of the trailer.

Before we left Pineville, I encountered a unique dilemma. I was in desperate need to empty my bowels, and there was absolutely nowhere to do it. With no other options, I climbed in the back, pulled the Naugahyde curtain for privacy, and did what I had to do in a Wal-Mart bag. After securely tying the offending package, I disposed of it in a ditch beside the truck. There were no trash barrels around, and I certainly wasn't going to ride around with a bag of human waste in the cab.

I felt guilty about littering Louisiana with a bag of shit, but I got back to the business of finishing my trip plan. As I sat in the driver's seat pecking away at my calculator, a pickup truck pulled ahead of me and stopped. A man with a burlap bag emerged from the vehicle and proceeded to pick up trash alongside the road. I realized, with horror, that he would soon make his way to my "gift."

I considered driving away, but my trip plan wasn't complete, so I just sat there squirming. While he couldn't have <u>known</u> I left the offending bag, it was sitting right next to my truck and it was, no doubt, still warm—he'd certainly be entitled to a suspicion!

I cringed as he approached the bag. He picked it up by the handles and, as he curiously inspected the mysterious contents, he crinkled his nose demurely—then knowingly. As he held the bag with a look of disgust, he slowly gazed in my direction. I immediately turned my attention to the map in my lap. I did not have the nerve to meet his indicting look. I would have been perfectly content for a crevasse to open in the earth and swallow me up. Despite my cowardice to return his look, I sincerely attempted a telepathic transmission of, "Sorry, dude."

After this embarrassing experience, we set out for Lake Charles. Lake Charles is the major cultural and educational center in Acadiana.[49] Acadiana is the official name given to the French Louisiana region that is home to a large Cajun population. Of the sixty-four parishes that make up Louisiana, twenty-two of them make up Acadiana.[50]

Because this was a hazardous materials load, I was required to watch a training film in Lake Charles before I picked up the load. Afterward, a black cloud of love bugs on I-10 bombarded my truck. I stopped at a truck stop to clean my windshield that was, ironically, Love's. The bugs were still as thick as fog as I walked across the parking lot to the store. I probably inhaled no less than two love bugs on my perilous trek, and I dug another out of my ear as I entered the store to escape the onslaught.

The manager of Love's watched from behind the fuel desk as I brushed the last of the bugs from my clothing.

"Hey man," I said, "I know this is Love's, but you've got to find a better way to advertise!"

"I'm gonna use that," he laughed.

The swarm of bugs eventually thinned, and we continued our journey. I was pulled in for a DOT inspection at a weigh station before I got out of Louisiana, but the officer found no violations. I continued on to the Mississippi Welcome Center on I-55 to spend the night.

Next day, it rained all the way through Mississippi, Tennessee, and Kentucky. We spent the night in Sonora, Kentucky, about 40 miles south of Louisville.

The rain continued on Wednesday all the way into Natrium. I had no trouble finding Natrium, but finding the correct gate at the PPG plant there was a different story. I had to do an awkward turn-around in a small parking lot after turning into the wrong entrance.

Natrium is just outside of Moundsville, West Virginia. Moundsville is the hometown of one of my old Navy buddies. He used to poke fun at his suburban hometown, but it seemed like a quaint, cozy little town to me. Moundsville is also the birthplace of Frank De Vol, an actor and composer who is probably best known for his composition of the theme song for *The Brady Bunch*.[51]

After delivering in Natrium, I went to the TA in nearby Wheeling to spend the night. I broke my credo and ate at the buffet on that evening. I promised myself not to do it again, lest I live up to the acronym: **B**ig **U**gly **F**at **F**uckers **E**ating **T**ogether.

Next morning, we picked up the next load in Triadelphia, West Virginia, which delivered to Prairie du Chien, Wisconsin. We made it to the Columbus, Ohio terminal for the night where I got my truck serviced and enjoyed a badly needed shower. I hoped to get on a homeward path after delivering in Wisconsin. Winter was rapidly approaching and driving in the northern states promised to be harrowing.

I stopped at a truck stop on the way to Prairie du Chien where I picked up a brochure for the Spam Museum. Yes, there actually is a Spam Museum in Austin, Minnesota. I wouldn't mind visiting, but I'd probably opt for a tee shirt instead of the meat-like product.

Later, I encountered an Amish family tooling along in a horse-drawn carriage on the opposite side of the road. The Amish populations in Pennsylvania, Ohio, and Indiana are well known, but Wisconsin is quickly becoming the state with the fourth highest Amish population. As populations and land prices increase in the eastern states, there is more motivation for families to move to less expensive, open areas of land.[52]

After delivering to Cabela's in Prairie du Chien, we got our next load assignment: from Clinton, Iowa to Fairburn, Georgia…then home.

Week 40: Georgia Chicken Coop

When we arrived at the shipper in Clinton, my assigned pre-loaded trailer was not in the yard. Someone, apparently, had fouled up my paperwork. With this being Sunday, no Shipping employees were there to correct it. Fortunately, a woman named Sherry had came in on her off day and was kind enough to address the problem. It took about an hour and a half, but Sherry corrected the gaffe and I was on my way. Encountering kind and generous people like that almost made me forget about the abundance of assholes I had to deal with on a daily basis…almost!

I went sixty miles before I found a truck stop with scales and, to my dismay, I saw that I was five thousand pounds heavy on the rear tandems. The standard procedure is to go back to the shipper for them to reload it when the weight is excessively out of proportion. However, I knew that no loading crew was working at the shipper on Sunday, and going back would ensure that I'd be stuck there until Monday. I managed to make the weight legal by sliding the tandems back. Disengaging the tandem-locking pin and leaving the trailer tire brakes engaged while pulling the truck forward accomplishes this. This causes the trailer to slide forward while the tires sit in place, thereby adjusting the weight distribution in relation to the axles.

My weight was legal now, but the rear tandems were all the way to the back. According to what I'd learned in orientation, Georgia's "bridge law" states that tandems cannot exceed 40 feet. Mine were <u>way</u> beyond that.

I called Brian and he said that if I weren't going to wait at the shipper, he'd recommend sliding them forward again before I got to Georgia. This would make me overweight in the rear again, but an overweight ticket costed less than an "over bridge" ticket. Besides, I only had to cross one weigh station in Georgia, and there was a good chance it would be closed. I considered the risk versus sitting idle at the shipper until Monday, and I decided to roll the dice.

After spending the night in Effingham, Illinois, I crossed two weigh stations in Illinois, one in Kentucky, and one in Tennessee. I had no problem at any of them. They didn't care about my bridge length as long as the weight was legal. I only needed to dodge one more bullet.

Just before I crossed the Georgia state line, I stopped and slid my tandems forward as Brian suggested. As I approached the Georgia weigh station, I prayed for it to be closed. "Chicken coop" is a slang term used by truckers to describe a weigh station. My heart sank when I saw the *Open* light brightly illuminated and watched the big rigs ahead of me herd into the chicken coop like lemmings. I knew my fate was sealed as I pulled onto the exit ramp.

When I rolled over the scales, an authoritative voice on the intercom boomed for me to bring all my paperwork inside. I gathered my license, medical card, log book, permits, and bills of lading for the load before I began a slow and deliberate death march toward the DOT building. As I entered, I watched the pudgy Georgia DOT officer lick his chops; this was the preamble to a devilishly good time for him.

I got an overweight ticket, and it doubled the rotund officer's delight when he told me the Georgia bridge law was now defunct.

"If you had just left your tandems alone," he guffawed, "you would have been fine."

As his face flushed with laughter, the loose skin beneath his jaw waddled like a chicken's neck. I attempted to contain my seething as I accepted the ticket from the pudgy little pullet, and got on my way.

I called Brian back to tell him what happened, and he was in shock. The Georgia bridge law was still on the books, and the company did not notify drivers of a change. Brian kept apologizing for giving me bad advice, but I told him not to worry about it—it wasn't his fault. I chose to roll the dice…and I lost.

Along with my newly acquired ticket, Kitty and I rolled into the Marietta terminal or, as it is affectionately referred to by some drivers, "The Prison." A ten-foot chain-link fence encloses the Marietta terminal, and tire spikes just past the fuel islands prevent drivers from backing out once they're in. To get out, the driver must swipe his fuel card in a scanner to open the rear gate. Half the time, the scanner doesn't work and the driver is trapped…hence, The Prison.

While at the terminal, I had a tire replaced and used the opportunity to go inside and meet my terminal manager, Dick, for the first time. On the phone, Dick's voice boomed in a rich and authoritative baritone. In person, Dick was a little old, hunchbacked man with thick glasses and coffee-tinged halitosis. This was going to severely disrupt my fantasies of punching him in the kisser.

We would spend the night at the terminal and deliver to Fairburn early in the morning. I hated searching for a place that I'd never been before in the darkness of night, but it often happened . The rain continued to fall from the gloomy gray skies, serving as a testament to the way this run had gone.

We left at 3am the next morning, and the Qualcomm directions sent me down a **dirt road** in Fairburn. I had to do a precarious turn-around in a motel parking lot, but I finally found the Purina plant, made the delivery, and set out for home in the pouring rain. We arrived in Scottsboro for three days of home time and, as usual, it seemed to end before it had started.

I reluctantly left on Friday to pick up a load in Guin, Alabama that delivered to Madison Heights, Michigan, a suburb of Detroit. The dock at the 3M plant in Guin was impossible. Ditches, other trucks and trailers, and a vast array of junk blocked my potential maneuvering space. I tried every conceivable angle to get into the dock to no avail. The shipper finally moved one of the trucks that blocked me, and then I docked with no problem. I was drenched in sweat when the merciful sound of the air brakes signaled the end of my ordeal. This was a nightmarish way to begin a road trip. After loading, we spent the night at a little truck stop just up the road in Hamilton, Alabama.

We left at 5:30am on Saturday and made it to the Pilot in Pendleton, Kentucky for the night. As I sat at the truck stop and listened to the rumble of diesel engines under the cover of night, I realized that the job still spawned a sense of adventure and offered a freedom that few other jobs could match. Despite the angst often attached to it, this was still a job like no other.

When I got out of the Navy in 1983, I briefly held a horrible job at a chicken processing plant. I recall looking into the cabs of the trucks at the break of dawn and wondering where the driver was going next. I never thought that, over twenty years later, someone might be peering into my cab and wondering the same thing. Trucking has plenty of pitfalls, but it certainly breaks up the monotony of a regular job. On this night, I liked my job.

Week 41: Detroit, Kalamazoo, and Buffalo Commons

We made it to the TA in Morgan, Michigan on Sunday, and we were lucky to get there early—it was already packed and filling up quickly. As the sun went down, I watched a Lot lizard scurry from truck to truck in search of clients. Unlike the haggard appearance worn by most lizards, this young black girl would have looked more appropriate with an American Literature book under her arm on a Community College campus rather than propositioning truckers.

It was still dark the next morning when we rolled into Madison Heights. I passed right by the customer because a tree cast a shadow over the lighted sign. Fortunately, I only had to make one turn around to find the place. The customer promised to cut down the offending tree since I was not the first driver to fall victim to its shadows. After delivery, we headed to Kalamazoo, Michigan for the next load.

Kalamazoo was originally a Native American name, although its exact origin is a source of debate. The unusual name has inspired many poets, authors, and songwriters to cite it in their works.[53] My first introduction to Kalamazoo occurred at the age of six while reading Dr. Seuss's *Horton Hatches the Egg*.

We waited over four hours in Kalamazoo for our load to be ready. During that time, I called the Safety Department manager, Broomhilde, to discuss my recent DOT inspection. We were supposed to get a $25 bonus for passing a DOT inspection, and I had yet to receive it.

As usual, Broomhilde was condescending and patronizing throughout the conversation. She always thought she knew what I was going to say before I said it and, consequently, often cut off my sentences and completed them for me. A word that rhymes with "ditch" entered my mind more than once, but I managed to refrain from verbally identifying her species.

After finally getting our load, we made it to a truck stop just across the Indiana state line on I-69 for the night. Gordonsville, Tennessee would be the destination for this load.

We headed out at 4am and found the interstate closed for construction around Daleville, Indiana. I lost my way on a county road detour and went all the way to Muncie before I corrected my bearings. A further delay occurred on US231 going into Tennessee from Kentucky. A multi-car accident held traffic at a standstill as I watched a bloody, unmoving body transported to a stretcher. It never got easier to view the aftermath of a crash.

In the months ahead, I would observe the aftermath of the worst traffic accident I've ever seen:

We sat idle on the Indianapolis bypass for over two hours as emergency personnel rushed to the scene. I could not see the site of the accident from where I sat, but its severity was apparent when a helicopter arrived to airlift crash victims. When the wreckage was cleared, I witnessed, with disbelief, the cars involved in the accident—they were barely identifiable as cars. Nothing remained of one of them except twisted metal and an untouched steering wheel that seemed to taunt motorists as they passed. Two flatbed straight trucks were required to remove the debris: one for what was left of the vehicle and another for all the pieces. It brought back somber memories of the day that changed Merlin's life forever, and I felt like no less of a man as the recollection forced me to wipe away a tear.

Despite the detour and delay, we made it to Gordonsville on time and spent the night at a truck stop in Lebanon, Tennessee. Our next load picked up in Clarksville, Tennessee for McCook, Nebraska.

Clarksville had the distinction of having the first and only bank in the world established and operated entirely by women.[54] During World War I, women's suffrage was becoming a major issue, and Clarksville women saw a need for banking independent of their husbands and fathers who were fighting. In response, the First Women's Bank of Tennessee was established in 1919.[55] Although the First Trust and Savings Bank of Clarksville absorbed it in 1926, it remains a unique historical milestone.

Loading at U.S. Zinc in Clarksville was a breeze. We were loaded and gone in less than half an hour. Thanks to the expediency of the shipper, we made it all the way to Kansas City for the night.

I slept in until 8am at the Kansas City terminal and decided to make it a short day. While driving through Kansas on I-70 west, there were signs inviting me to "See live rattlesnakes," "Pet the baby pig," and "See the largest Prairie Dog in the world." As tempting as it sounded, we forged ahead and spent the night in Wakeeney, Kansas.

Wakeeney is known as "The Christmas City of the High Plains." Since 1950, Wakeeney hosts an ornate Christmas lighting display that now includes over six thousand lights and a thirty-five foot Christmas tree in the center of town. The tree is ceremonially lit the Saturday night after Thanksgiving.[56] [57]

Wakeeney's prosperity in the late 1800's was primarily based on land sales. The Western Kansas World newspaper in 1886 listed about twenty firms attached to the sale of land. The following is an ad that appeared in The Western Kansas World in 1886:

> *LIE, STEAL, DRINK, AND SWEAR. When you lie, let it be in bed, on your claim. When you steal, let it be away from bad company. When you drink, drink moderately. When you swear, swear that your Land Agent shall be no other than McKnight and Whittsill, Land and Loans.*

The delivery to McCook went fine, even though it turned out to be a lengthy live unload instead of the quick "drop and hook" I'd been expecting. We then sat in the drop yard for over an hour waiting for another load offering.

McCook, Nebraska plays host to an annual event called the Buffalo Commons Storytelling Festival. The seeds for the festival's birth were planted in 1987 when Dr. Frank Popper of Rutgers University and his wife Deborah advanced a theory that the arid Great Plains would lose almost all their people within the coming quarter-century.[58] Because this area would continue to de-populate, age, and face further economic decline, the New Jersey professors asserted that the Great Plains should become a massive ecological reserve which they would call "Buffalo Commons."

McCook and its neighbors took it personally when the Poppers implied that this part of the country should never have been settled. The dominant sentiment among southwest Nebraskans was that the Poppers should return to New Jersey and let them continue their persevering ways. McCook's town leaders decided it was time to accentuate the positive. The tales of southwest Nebraska deserved telling, and a storytelling festival was the perfect vehicle. As a final rebuttal to the Poppers, McCook chose the name of Buffalo Commons Storytelling Festival.

Despite the merit contained in many of the Poppers' predictions, an article by Florence Williams in High Country News states that the amiable Poppers were content to ride a manure spreader in a centennial parade down the main street of Gwinner, North Dakota. Thirteen years after they first pitched their idea of turning the ailing plains into a vast Buffalo Commons, Frank Popper happily says, "We have gone from being East Coast academic Martians to being, well, almost local."[59]

We picked up our next load in Sterling, Colorado. At the shipper, I succeeded in getting innumerable sticky burrs attached to my pants and, as a bonus, at least seven or eight flies boarded the truck for a ride back to Nebraska. The flies and the burrs tormented me for most of the way. I made an appeal to Kitty to catch the flies, but she seemed content to just play with them.

Shortly after crossing back into Nebraska on I-80, I saw a whirlwind of tumbleweeds and debris spinning above the interstate. The cone whirled twenty to thirty feet in the air. I had never seen a dust devil before, but this was a healthy one. Like a tornado, a dust devil is a rotating updraft. Dust devils are ordinarily harmless, but they can still pack a scary wallop. While tornadoes form as an updraft attached to a wall cloud at the back of a thunderstorm, dust devils form as an updraft under sunny conditions in fair weather.

The devil whirled vigorously in the right-hand lane, and it rocked the entire truck with violent authority as I passed through it. Not only had I now seen a dust devil, I had driven smack through the middle of one!

We shut down for the evening at a truck stop in Big Springs, Nebraska. Our present load was going to Memphis, Tennessee. I called Brian and told him I was about to go searching for Elvis.

Week 42: RC Cola and Moon Pie

I finally washed my truck on Sunday in Ozora, Missouri. I almost forgot that it was actually shiny beneath all the crud. We made it to the Petro in West Memphis, Arkansas for the night. Not only was it a massive clusterfuck, they charged a ten dollar parking fee for the privilege of entering the fray. Truck stops that charge parking fees are more common in the northeast, but I try to give any of them as little business as possible.

The parking spots at the West Memphis Petro were crammed close to one another, and I almost grazed the mirror of another truck as I attempted to squeeze in. I was tempted to go inside for a meal in the restaurant after the stressful ordeal. Although Petro's Iron Skillet is, in my opinion, the best restaurant of the major truck stop chains, I decided to forgo it because of the greedy parking fee. It was just as well. I noticed that I'd gained a few pounds, and cutting back on restaurant food seemed to be in order. Either that or I should peruse Victoria's Secret for a bra that compliments my *Trucking Ain't For Sissies* tee shirt.

I called the customer on Monday morning before going to Memphis to ask about their tricky dock. A Qualcomm message warned that three prior trucks got their trailer dollies stuck there and needed a tow truck for freedom. I saw the potential problem when I arrived. The dock angled downward and a large concrete hump separated the docking area from the street. Any attempt to pull into the street to straighten the docking maneuver presented a genuine possibility of getting the dollies lodged on the hump. The solution was to nail the dock off the 45° angle maneuver using no "pull-up." It required three attempts, but I managed to dock without hanging on the hump.

We picked up the next load in Grenada, Mississippi; a comparatively easy place in which to maneuver. Hayti, Missouri was our resting place for the night. We would deliver to Lawrence, Kansas on Wednesday.

I felt better on Tuesday after sleeping late and taking a long rest stop in Kingdom City, Missouri. While in Kingdom City, I walked over to a souvenir plaza called Nostalgiaville, USA. It offered various memorabilia, mostly from the 50's and 60's. After browsing for almost an hour, I walked away with a framed picture of the Beverly Hillbillies.

Afterward, we went to the Kansas City terminal to shut down for the day where I parked next to a driver yapping vigorously on his cell phone. When I returned from the restroom inside the terminal, he was still jabbering with fervor.

Kansas City was unseasonably hot, so I cranked up to cool off the truck. Once I did, the chattering driver waved for me to shut it off.

Yeah! I'm going to sit here and bake so he can yap on the cell phone!

I merely shook my head and motioned him to go elsewhere.

We arrived in Lawrence on Wednesday morning for the delivery. Downtown Lawrence's lively atmosphere hinges on a vast assortment of restaurants, bars, galleries, shops, and music venues. Lawrence grabbed national attention in the early 1980's because of the television movie, *The Day After*. The movie depicted what would happen to average Americans if the United States came under nuclear attack.

Lawrence suffered another fictional nuclear disaster in 2006 when a nuclear blast destroyed the city in the television series, *Jericho*. In reality, however, the city of Lawrence has an extensive tunnel system beneath Massachusetts Street and the University of Kansas designed as a nuclear attack shelter.[60]

Once again, I had to back into the customer's dock off the street in the midst of heavy traffic. Under the circumstances, it went well this time. I went to a small coffee shop in the downtown area to kill time as the truck was unloaded. When I returned, I sat and watched many well-dressed business people pass in front of the truck with tightly gripped leather briefcases in tow and expressions of urgency on their faces. Most of them paid me no mind, but a few offered a confused gaze as if they observed an alien. I rested contently on the assumption that their idea of success and happiness might be different from mine. Of the handful of wealthy and "successful" people I've known, most were every bit as dysfunctional as the rest of us and in some cases, even more so. I was learning to measure success in terms of personal fulfillment and happiness rather than in material gain. A grin crept across my face with the knowledge that I would not trade places with any of them for…well, a million bucks!

After Lawrence, we picked up the next load on the Kansas side of Kansas City to deliver to Decatur, Alabama with a stop-off in Huntsville. This run would give me the opportunity for a 34-hour restart at home.

The billboards for Ann's Bra Shop on I-70 between Kansas City and St. Louis always gave me a chuckle.

"Bra problems?" they unfailingly inquired.

When we got to the Flying J in Warrenton, Missouri, I saw that one of my trailer door latches had popped loose. Under no circumstances is a driver ever supposed to break the seal on a loaded trailer, but I could not continue this run with my trailer door in this condition. In my experience, 90% of customers never check the seal—they just tell the driver to remove it. Most companies who actually do monitor the seals, like Starbucks, use a bolt seal that requires bolt cutters to remove.

I called dispatch for advice, and they told me I'd either have to continue with the door ajar or return all the way to Kansas to have it resealed. Neither option was acceptable. I made a bold decision to break the seal, open the door, correct the problem, and reseal it with a generic company seal. When I arrived in Huntsville, I explained the entire situation to the customer. They actually thanked me for taking the initiative and not delaying their shipment. My decision was a risky one, but it worked out nicely this time—the customer was happy, and that's all my company needed to know.

On the way home to Scottsboro, I was caught in a forty-five minute backup on I-24 around Bell Buckle, Tennessee. This oddly named city hosts the annual RC Cola and Moon Pie festival. These two Southern classics became a popular treat among mine workers in the early 1900's. The RC Cola and

Moon Pie combination gained popularity as "the working man's lunch", and took its place as a Southern tradition.

No one really knows what inspired the marriage between Royal Crown Cola and Moon Pie, but by the late 1950's, the combination was highly popular throughout the South. RC Cola was less expensive that its competitors and Moon Pies were significantly larger than they are today. Consequently, you could buy the two for about a dime and enjoy a sugar-filled extravaganza.[61]

The stop-off delivery in Huntsville went fine, but I was not so fortunate in Decatur. Decatur, Alabama is home to one of the Meow Mix production facilities, and a sign reading, "Decatur: Home of Meow Mix" can be seen atop a building from the Tennessee River bridge. Decatur is also home to the first wave pool ever built in the United States at the Point Mallard Aquatic Center.[62]

My directions to Home Depot in Decatur were lacking, and I had to turn around in a residential area where a low-hanging branch broke off my radio antenna. I stopped at a convenience store to ask a local woman for directions, but the updated instructions lacked clarity as well. I finally pulled into a shopping center and luckily, saw a city police officer sitting there. He did one better than providing accurate directions—he gave me a police escort to Home Depot! Unlike the beer-bellied Georgia DOT officer who almost had an orgasm giving me a ticket, this officer helped to restore my faith that all cops weren't assholes. While it's true that some cops take advantage of truckers being an easy target, it's nice to know there are others who are genuinely good people.

I got back to Scottsboro after midnight for a glorious thirty-four hours at home. We would go back out on Sunday for two more weeks and then, hopefully, come back home for three or four days.

Detour: The Lonely Road

The aroma of a truck stop restaurant is curiously comforting. The smell of greasy breakfast food and stale cigarettes blends perfectly with the lively conversation of truckers. An overweight woman sits on a counter stool exchanging profanely-riddled diatribe with a man in a flannel shirt and a CAT baseball cap. A balding man with flush cheeks listens intently as he lights up a third or fourth Marlboro, awaiting the next opportunity to heave a mighty guffaw. Teasing insults flow as smoothly as genuine kindness among truckers, and most are grateful for a few moments of story swapping and interaction among peers.

Loneliness is, often, the immediate response to what makes life as a trucker difficult. While a scenario similar to the previous one can still be found in truck stops, they are becoming increasingly rare.

Truck stops were once the hub of a trucker's business and social network. In the days before cell phones and Qualcomms, truckers contacted dispatch on a pay phone in the driver's lounge or simply hung out until it was time to go down the road again. In this environment, business contacts were made, stories were shared, and friendships were developed.

Today, truckers are losing the time to interact with other drivers in a social atmosphere that used to be a staple of the industry.[63] With cell phones, text messaging, refrigerators and microwaves in the trucks, and the gradual disappearance of Mom & Pop truck stops, drivers often have limited time to socialize. With the ever-changing rules and regulations of both the DOT and individual trucking companies, and expectations of faster deliveries, time management usually wins out over social activity.

Trucking is unlike any other lifestyle. On any given day, it can be the greatest job on earth, and the next day, cracking yourself in the head with a sledgehammer seems joyous in comparison. It is often an emotional roller-coaster ride that spawns the desire for simple human interaction. Few other jobs involve as much private thought as trucking. Each day holds many hours of solitary confinement.

The solitary life of a trucker is hard enough for a single man or woman, but it becomes an even greater challenge for someone with a family. Not surprisingly, the divorce rate among truckers is much higher than the national average. In an article by Kevin Bates in the Topeka Capital-Journal, truck driver Dale Hutchens states:

"You gotta be some sort of a nomad, a loner, to do this job. We all want to be with our families, especially during the holidays, but that's the life I chose."

While many people were at home with family, opening gifts beneath the Christmas tree, Hutchens ate lunch at Roost Family Restaurant, a Topeka truck stop, and prepared for a northward trip.

"It's a way of life," says Hutchens, "you either accept it or you don't."

Hutchens still visits his Grandmother when he travels to the east. This makes holidays on the road more bearable, but he still has a lot of time to think about his nine-year-old daughter, Megan.

"I saw her a little bit yesterday, but I'm not going to be able to see her today. I gave her some Lego sets. I think about her constantly."

For Hutchens and most other long-haul truckers, driving is a lifelong marriage to the road.

For me, the solitude of the road provides a mixed blessing. To observe a quiet and peaceful West Virginia sunrise while Kitty sleeps quietly in the passenger's seat has a way of making me feel at peace with the world. At other times, I sorely miss the human interaction among co-workers in an ordinary job. The road is a mixture of excitement, serenity, loneliness, and stress. As long-haul truckers, the best we can do is try and make a home for ourselves on the road.

Most truckers use cell phones to stay in contact with family and friends. Broadband services are also available for Internet access. A driver can join mailing lists, chat groups, and develop cyber-friendships. It also helps to bring things from home to make the rig feel closer to home. Familiar music and photos and a refrigerator stocked with some favorite foods from home offer a consoling diversion. It is also fun to snap pictures with a digital camera and send them to family and friends, or post them online, allowing them to share in some of your adventures. A webcam and a free video chat service like Skype even allows the driver more personal interaction with family. Some drivers even take online classes on the road. While the rigors of road life would make it challenging to devote proper time and study to a college-level course, I firmly believe that if a person wants something badly enough, he or she will find a way to make it happen. If all else fails, a driver might consider teaming. Teaming has many pros and cons, but it might be an option worth considering for drivers whom loneliness proves too heavy a cross to bear.

Finally, a pet can be an indispensable companion on the road. For me, Kitty is my Rock of Gibraltar against loneliness. Unfortunately, more companies are eliminating (or already have eliminated) pet policies for company drivers. However, a handful of companies still allow drivers to bring along a furry friend. I cannot imagine being on the road without Kitty.

Kitty came into my life almost twelve years ago. As an abandoned and dying stray kitten, I paid the vet to nurse her back to health and then claimed her as my own. Kitty has remained with me through job loss, the death of a loved one, relocation, breakups, career change, and many other trying times. Through it all, she has never expected anything but food and love. Her round paunch proves that she gets plenty of the former, and my commitment to my loyal pet gives her plenty of the latter. As long as Kitty is around, I'll never work for a trucking company with a "No Pets" policy.

Kitty has even offered subtle life lessons on dealing with loneliness on the road. On a beautiful Saturday morning in Tulsa, I watched as Kitty hung her head out the window and sniffed the morning air. The worries and stresses of daily mundane existence shortly evaporated as I watched the twitching pink nose of a small animal soak in the aroma of life. Loneliness was the farthest thing from my mind as I digested the simple and profound lesson that Kitty taught.

Author's Note: Some things put forth in this article have changed since I first sat down to write it. When I originally wrote this essay in 2007, many truck stops still allowed smoking in the restaurants. Now, almost none still do. Whether that is a good thing or a bad thing depends, I suppose, on whether or not you smoke. Also, Roost Family Restaurant is now, sadly, closed. Smartphone technology has also improved dramatically since this time and iPad and tablet technology gives drivers yet more options to stay connected with family. Taking online courses has never been easier than it is now with the growing popularity of free MOOCs (Massive Open Online Courses). A properly motivated individual can now take quality online courses from an increasing list of top-notch universities without spending a dime. My personal favorite is Coursera.org.

Week 43: Macon Whoopee

I could not muster the motivation to leave on Sunday, so we spent an extra day at home and left on Monday morning. Our first run was a repeat of one we'd done before: Gadsden, Alabama to Homerville, Georgia. I stopped for the day at the Pilot in Tallapoosa, Georgia, having no desire to deal with Atlanta's rush hour. Homerville went smoothly, and then we got a run from Macon, Georgia to Marietta, Pennsylvania.

Macon was home to a hockey team called the Macon Whoopees. The Whoopees played in the Southern Hockey League in 1973. Despite a brief flash of national publicity because of the nickname, the team disbanded in mid-season due to poor attendance. The Whoopee (without the plural "s") appeared again in 1996 where they played in the Central Hockey League and the East Coast Hockey League until 2002.[64] The logo changed from a fig leaf to a whooping crane with a bee on the blade of its hockey stick. The "bird and the bee" were intended as a play on the team name. I still worked in the television industry during this time, and I recall the resurrection of the Macon Whoopee. It was at least three months before any sportscaster or anchor could say the team name with a straight face.

After spending the entire day on country roads, I almost got out and kissed the asphalt of I-20 when we finally got there. I bore the heavy weight of fatigue when we stopped at a small Circle K truck stop in Thomson, Georgia for the night.

On Wednesday, Kitty and I passed through seven states. We spent the night at the TA in Greencastle, Pennsylvania that had IdleAire hookups for the trucks. IdleAire provides in-cab services to truckers via centralized systems at select truck stops across the country. The technology is called Advanced Travel Center Electrification (ATE). A distinctive yellow tube that hooks into the door window of the truck delivers the ATE services.[65] The interactive panel at the end of the tube provides heating and air-conditioning, phone service, Internet connectivity, television, movies-on-demand, and 110-volt electrical outlets. The services come at an hourly rate, and a ten-dollar window adapter is the only item needed before receiving services.

While some drivers give grand testimonials for IdleAire, others consider it a rip off. I used the service once and found it to work nicely. It kept the truck toasty warm on a cold winter night with no idling. However, the hourly rate coupled with the many "extras" that come at additional cost can quickly mount a substantial bill. Depending on how many of the tempting extras are purchased, the rate can easily run higher than a motel room.

As Brian puts it, "With a motel room, you get a shower and a crapper to boot!"

While IdleAire might be a good idea, it doesn't seem cost effective for a driver whose company does not reimburse the cost. Also, the IdleAire staff is often annoying and intrusive to a tired driver who does not purchase their service. The large yellow tubes also make the truck stop resemble a McDonald's playland.

Author's Note: IdleAire filed for bankruptcy in 2008 and officially closed for business in January of 2010. They have since been revived as IdleAir and are re-emerging at truck stops across the country. I never used the revamped service, but I sincerely hope the staff is less intrusive to drivers than the previous incarnation.

I altered my route plan again when I saw the company's directions routing me over the South Mountains on a U.S. highway. I did not know how bad it was, but I was taking no chances on another Gatlinburg-like drama at midnight. This load delivered at 2am.

After running hard for two days straight and getting up before midnight after only a couple of hours sleep, I was feeling the results of the deprivation. Fortunately, parking was available at the customer in Marietta, so I parked for about three hours after delivery for a nap. Afterward, we picked up a load in Hanover, Pennsylvania.

Hanover is home to the national pretzel and snack food distribution center, Snyder's of Hanover. These products are also found throughout Europe, in Southeast Asia, and in the Middle East. Hanover is also home to The Famous Hot Wiener restaurant where, as claimed in their ads, "We've served our famous wieners since 1923."[66]

On the way to Hanover, US30 seemed to be nothing but a series of small towns and red lights. The Hanover was slated for Kansas City with a stop-off in Hazelwood, Missouri. After loading, we made it to the TA in Wheeling, West Virginia for the night.

It would not be entirely accurate to call the security guard in Hazelwood a jerk, so I'll just call him what he was—an asshole! When I arrived, he ran to my truck as if his pants were ablaze and yelled adamantly that I was blocking the driveway. I surveyed the surroundings and noted that, on this Sunday, the entire facility was as deserted as an Arizona ghost town.

"Who am I blocking?" I inquired.

It required less than a minute to conduct my business inside, but the guard maintained his pugnacious rants the entire time. Afterward, I leisurely ambled back to my truck, just to watch his veins bulge. The "traffic flow" was still non-existent.

We arrived at the Kansas City terminal at 2pm where I showered, cooked dinner, and watched TV until it was time to make the final delivery on the other side of town. We returned to the terminal after delivery where I allowed Kitty to roam around outside and eat grass, or "Kitty salad." A hard day coupled with a dipshit security guard had left me in a bad mood, but watching Kitty derive such pleasure from a pure communion with nature made it impossible to stay angry.

Week 44: Jersey Manners and the Flopeye Fish Festival

I finally got a load offering from Topeka, Kansas to Keasbey, New Jersey. Each time I visit the Garden State, I tend to experience a healthy dose of New Jersey manners. While I'm sure there are many agreeable people in New Jersey, I have had my share of personal dealings with the other kind. My first sampling of "the other kind" happened at a travel plaza off the New Jersey Turnpike.

An impatient janitor appealed to go past me as I stood in a long line waiting to purchase an over-priced breakfast sandwich. Instead of saying, "Excuse me," he just clucked his tongue for me to get out of the way. This was such an unbelievable display of rudeness that I couldn't even get mad…I merely laughed aloud.

The New Jersey load would not be ready until Monday, so we spent all of Sunday sitting at a rainy Kansas City terminal.

We arrived at the Payless Distribution Center in Topeka at 6am on Monday only to find out the freight would not be ready until after noon. I called dispatch and they switched me to a Memphis load. Although this was a shorter run, I shed no tears about avoiding New Jersey. It rained all day again, but we made it to Hayti, Missouri for the night.

After delivery in Memphis, I had to do a short shag run. I detest shags! They are time-consuming, hard work, and the small amount of extra money does not compensate for the effort. I took a run to Columbus, Ohio after the vile shag and spent the night at the North 40 truck stop in Holladay, Tennessee. Here, I decided to splurge by enjoying a piece of chocolate fried pie.

We got to Columbus on Wednesday and, for the first time in a while, I had to blindside into the dock with no pull-up room. This time, I did it with less effort than in most of my previous attempts. I finally seemed to be getting better at challenging maneuvers.

After delivery, we went to the Columbus terminal to spend the night. We'd pick up a load at Kal Kan in Columbus in the morning that goes to Columbia, South Carolina. I could have taken a run to Nevada, and I probably would have if I weren't trying to get home on Monday. Dispatch often offered an enticing long run when the driver's home request drew near.

After a restless night's sleep, I got up at 2am and drove right past Kal Kan. I despise looking for an unfamiliar place in the dark, but it is often necessary. While driving through Cincinnati, I found myself humming the familiar tune to *WKRP*. I cannot help myself—I do it every time.

With over 40,000 pounds of dog food in tow, the mountains of the Virginias were slow and tedious. I only drove five hundred miles, but it felt like a lot more. We endured a further delay waiting in a long fuel line at Love's in Max Meadows, Virginia. Tempers among some of the drivers ran short in the midst of the chaos. A driver with a Russian accent rudely attempted to hurry me up. I politely (well, not entirely politely) told him he would have to wait until my business was complete.

Because of today's delays, I felt I'd be cutting it close to deliver legally. I told dispatch that I would deliver in the morning. This load was on an open-ended schedule, so it did not present a problem. We shut down about forty miles from the customer in Great Falls, South Carolina.

On Memorial Day weekend of each year, Great Falls hosts an annual Flopeye Fish Festival. More than seventy-five years ago, a local merchant often sat in front of his general store and fell asleep in his chair. One day, three women passed by and one of them blurted, "Who is that flop-eyed old man?"

Several bystanders heard her and the news made its way to Rob Mebane, the president of Republic Cotton Mills. Mebane thought that "Flopeye" was a proper name for that part of town, so mill management promoted the name, and it took hold. People still enjoy saying they have been to Flopeye.[67]

The delivery to Columbia went as planned, and then we got a load from Anderson, South Carolina back to Columbus, Ohio. Dispatch promised they'd get me home out of Columbus.

We endured a two-hour traffic backup on I-26 in North Carolina, and I was tired and grumpy by the time we shut down for the night in Dandridge, Tennessee. The backup killed my plans to go farther today. Shortly after parking, dispatch sent me a pre-planned load to get me home out of Columbus.

Typically, I am grateful for a rare home pre-plan, but this one was very tightly scheduled. In order to do it on time and legally, I'd have to bend the rules to the breaking point, forgo getting a shower in the morning, and discard any inkling of a good night's sleep. This almost seemed like they were setting me up to fail. My cranky mood did not improve. However, I resolved to do whatever it took to pull it off—I wanted to go home! The walls of the truck have a way of closing in after a certain amount of time.

We rolled out at 2am on Saturday morning and drove non-stop to Columbus from Dandridge. I accomplished this by exercising a Zen-like strength of will on my bladder. Thanks to the triumph of meditation over caffeine, we made it to Columbus with time to spare. Afterward, we picked up a load in Cincinnati. It goes to McDonough, Georgia…then home sweet home!

I was tired, dirty, and still cranky at the end of the day, but a smile involuntarily crept across my face as I reflected on the challenges thrown in my path by this crazy job. In my old TV job, I never knew the stress and aggravation of blindsiding a 53-foot van into a small dock with no room to maneuver while my bladder screamed for relief. I neither knew the sense of invigoration that went along with actually pulling it off. My TV job never put me in a position where I was stuck in the snow in the middle of nowhere with no signal on my cell phone to call for help. It neither gave me the sense of accomplishment that comes with rising to the challenge of a day fraught with danger and impossible odds.

The smile plastered on my face was there because I was no longer doing something that sucked the joy of living from my soul. Despite the often hellish nature of trucking, my smile remained, and I counted my blessings…and then screwed the lid back on the pee jug.

Week 45: Silly Four-Wheelers and Squeaky Cheese

We started at 7:30am Sunday morning because I was unable to urge my body out of the sleeper when the alarm rang at 6am. A four-wheeler almost gave me a heart attack on I-75 in Tennessee when he jumped ahead of me off an entry ramp and subsequently slammed on his brakes. If there had been any traffic in the left lane beside me, I could not have avoided plowing into his rear. I was so pissed off when I passed him that I maintained a continuous blast of the road horn while I forced him to the shoulder with a maneuver affectionately known as a "New York Lane Change."

We spent the night at the Marietta terminal, a.k.a. "The Prison." I anxiously awaited four days at home after delivery to McDonough the next morning.

As usual, home time passed far too quickly, and it was difficult to muster the motivation to leave again on Friday in the midst of a pouring rainstorm. Kitty and I sucked it up and went anyway. Our first load was going to Fridley, Minnesota.

As we were tooling along on the westbound side of I-24 in Tennessee, a brown mini-van on the eastbound side lost control and careened across the median directly in front of me. I feared that it would hurl itself directly into my path but, fortunately, it regained traction and remained on the median. I am confident, however, that the episode caused me to release a few drops of coffee into my Spiderman boxer shorts.

It came as no surprise when the company had no directions available for the customer in Fridley. Instead of calling dispatch for instructions, I called the customer directly. Based on experience, it would be easier to pull a wisdom tooth with a pair of tweezers than to persuade dispatch to go out of their way to find directions not already in the system. The company frowned on drivers calling customers or shippers directly, but they were usually happy to help—unlike the dispatch office, for whom making an extra phone call was, apparently, as harrowing a task for them as putting toothpaste back into the tube.

We made it to the Pilot in Paducah, Kentucky for the night after driving all day in the rain. Kitty seemed happy to be back on the road. It's probably because she knew daily treats awaited her and, more often than not, a bit of whatever I was eating.

I awoke Saturday morning shivering in a freezing truck. The Opti-Idle unit was not functioning properly. Opti-Idle is an in-cab thermostat that allows the driver to set the desired temperature, and the truck turns itself on and off to maintain that temperature while reducing idle time and saving fuel. Every fifteen to thirty minutes, an alarm sounds for five seconds, then the truck cranks. Some drivers complain they cannot get a good night's sleep with the truck shutting on and off throughout the night, but it has never bothered me. In this case, however, I was slowly losing air pressure when the truck was off. When the air pressure goes below 60psi, a low-level air alarm blasts with the annoying velocity of a submarine Klaxon. Brian says that I probably have a bad fan hub and will require shop time. For now, I had the unenviable choice of leaving the truck off and freezing, or continually being awakened by the alarm.

Upon defrosting my bones, I got going and made it to the TA in Janesville, Wisconsin for the night. I allowed myself to indulge in one of my favorite treats—Wisconsin Cheese Curds. Cheese curds are sometimes referred to as "Squeaky Cheese" because a defining characteristic of fresh curds is a squeak against the teeth when bitten.[68] I often buy a couple of bags of curds when I come to Wisconsin, but they tend to lose their squeak after a couple of days. Kitty likes cheese curds too—and she doesn't seem to mind if they squeak or not.

Week 46: Darth Vader and the World's Largest Truck Stop

We made it to Hudson, Wisconsin on Sunday, just across the river from Minneapolis/St. Paul. We were fortunate to get a parking spot at the TA there because it is usually full and congested.

We arose early Monday morning and delivered to another CVS store in Fridley. Mercifully, this one was not as difficult as the one in Niantic. However, we waited for almost two hours before unloading began. Then, another truck snagged the spot where I was going to park after delivery. Now, I had nowhere to park to await the next load offering. Dispatch said it might take some time, so we went back to the TA in Hudson. For all I knew, we'd be sitting all day, and I did not want to spend it sitting in a mall parking lot.

We finally got a load offering and, as luck would have it, Hudson was 35 miles in the opposite direction from the shipper. Our load was at the 3M plant in Forest City, Iowa.

Forest City Community Schools operates a wind turbine that provides 60% of the energy for all city schools. The wind turbine started as a physics project, and it began producing in January of 1999. Forest City also claims to be the smallest town in the United States with its own YMCA.[69] The load was not ready when we arrived in Forest City and I was out of hours by the time we got it at 7pm. We spent the night at the shipper. To my dismay, we would be going to Chicago again. I made a vow to watch for low viaducts this time.

We got up at 4am to be greeted by a howling, frosty wind that cut through my clothing like a machete. The frigid air punished my body when I got out to unhook from my empty trailer and hook to the loaded one. While I am not an advocate of working in the blistering heat of summer, I prefer it to cold weather. My body ceases to cooperate with my mind in sub-zero temperatures. After playing a round of "joust and parry" with dispatch, they rescheduled my Chicago appointment to a more reasonable time.

I saw someone dressed as Darth Vader at a truck stop in Walcott, Iowa, and then I remembered that it was Halloween. Days on the road tended to overlap and merge. Friday or Saturday was no different from Monday or Tuesday, and holidays had little meaning. A trucker often recognizes only two distinctions: road time and home time.

Walcott's interchange on I-80 is home to an enormous complex of restaurants, motels, and truck stops, including the Iowa 80 truck stop, which is the world's largest. Set on a 220-acre plot of land, the Iowa 80 is four times bigger than the average truck stop and two and a half times larger than Disneyland. The Iowa 80 gets five thousand visitors daily and has a staff of four hundred and fifty employees. It has everything from the basics of food and fuel to truck washes, a truck museum, a movie theater, and even a dentist.[70]

We shut down for the night in Dixon, Illinois, the boyhood home of former President Ronald Reagan.[71] During his teen years, Reagan served as a lifeguard along the banks of Dixon's Rock River.

We arrived in Chicago the next day with plenty of time to spare. It went much better this time. The customer refused twenty boxes of scrub brushes due to some minor damage on the boxes. I called the company to find out what to do with them and they told me to bring them to the Ottawa terminal. This was fine with me—it gave me a chance to have the truck's Opti-Idle repaired.

There was nowhere to park at the laughingly tiny terminal, so I dropped my trailer at a nearby truck stop and bob-tailed back to the terminal. Fortunately, the boxes of scrub brushes were small enough to load into the cab.

I had dinner at Cracker Barrel while waiting for my truck to be repaired, and then went back to the truck stop to spend the night. A Triple X adult arcade was just across from where I parked. As I sat and watched patrons enter and leave, I grew amused by the various behaviors. Some glanced about nervously, as if they were on a covert mission while others walked in with bluster and pride as if they owned the place.

I woke up five minutes before the alarm rang and responded with a resounding "Shit!" I hated to wake up just a few minutes before the alarm went off. Our next load offering was from Kewanee, Illinois to Indianola, Mississippi.

Kewanee is acknowledged as the Hog Capital of the World, and it holds an annual Hog Days Festival every Labor Day weekend.[72] The title of Hog Capital dates to 1948 when Frank Preston Johnson of Kewanee introduced a resolution into the 66th Illinois General Assembly. The following is an excerpt from Mr. Johnson's speech:

> "And you, my colleagues from the great city of Chicago, who grunted the loudest during the reading of this resolution, you in your innocence may cherish the delusion that you have little in common with the Illinois hog. I assure you that you do—PLENTY! Every city must have some economic justification for its existence. That was true in the ancient past, and it is true today.
>
> Ships made Carthage
>
> The wars made Rome,
>
> Beer built Milwaukee,
>
> Gold made Nome,
>
> Cotton built Atlanta,
>
> The harbor made New York,
>
> But good old Chicago
>
> Was built on pork!"[73]

The shipper in Kewanee loaded us in record time, and we made it to a truck stop in Ozora, Missouri for the night. I considered going through the truck wash, but sleep proved a more attractive alternative.

I got up at 3am on Friday with the intention of going all the way to Indianola. However, by the time I got to Winona, Mississippi, my enthusiasm was gone and I stopped for the day.

I ate at a mobile home converted to a restaurant across from the Pilot truck stop. To my utter dismay, they had no biscuits to compliment my breakfast. Heck, it was blasphemous to have a Southern breakfast with no biscuits! To add insult to injury, the waitress was rude and unfriendly. I resolved to check my map when I returned to the truck to ensure I was in Mississippi, and not New Jersey.

We delivered to Indianola on Saturday morning where, seeing no one inside the guard shack, I rolled right past. The guard, who had apparently been hiding under the desk, ran out in a rage. He stomped up to my window as mad as a hippo with a hernia, but when I convinced him it was an honest mistake, he began to calm down.

There was only one slot in the drop yard to park a loaded trailer, and I incensed another driver by getting to it before him. I had pissed off two people in less than five minutes without even trying. Imagine what I could accomplish with a focused effort!

I finished in Indianola without enraging a third person, and then we went to Grenada, Mississippi for the next load. We shut down for the night at the TA in Earle, Arkansas. Other than inadvertently pissing off two people, this had been a good day.

Week 47: Toad Suck Park and Beer Nuts

I got a welcome laugh on a rainy day as I passed Toad Suck Park at exit 129B on I-40 in Arkansas. The legend behind Toad Suck is that it was a favorite place for bargemen, traveling the Arkansas River, to pull over and drink rum and moonshine. They are said to have "sucked on bottles until they swelled up like toads."[74]

Passing Toad Suck inspired a reminiscence of some of the more uniquely named places I have encountered in my travels. Among the more memorable are Intercourse, Alabama; Flush, Kansas; Hell for Certain, Kentucky; Square Butt, Missouri; Big Butt, North Carolina; Cumming, Georgia and Climax, Georgia; Hog Jaw, Arkansas; Two Egg, Florida; Stinking Creek, Tennessee and Big Ugly Creek, West Virginia. The Frog City truck stop in Rayne, Louisiana offers an entrée of frog legs or a frog burger. And if dirty laundry hampers your resolve, you can wash it at Suds Ur' Duds in Corinth, Mississippi.

The rainy day in Arkansas dampened my mood when I noticed the windshield still leaking. The Ottawa shop said they'd replaced the seal, yet the leak remained. I "rolled & dripped" my way to Sallisaw, Oklahoma where we spent the night at a Mom & Pop truck stop.

Sallisaw derived its name from the French word "salaiseau" meaning salt provisions. Salt deposits along the stream in this area furnished salt used by buffalo hunters and early settlers to preserve meat. Evidence of old salt kettles can still be found in Sequoyah County.[75] [76]

Monday's delivery to Tulsa went fine, but then we sat at the Flying J all day before getting a load offering to Romeoville, Illinois, a suburb of Chicago. After loading at the Kimberly-Clark plant in Jenks, Oklahoma, I was out of hours. The shipper refused to allow me to park there overnight, so I had to look elsewhere. I remembered seeing an old, abandoned Wal-Mart building on the way in, so I went back there to park. A rapping on the window roused me from sleep at 11pm, and a police officer informed me that I could not park there. The officer, an older man, apparently recognized my fatigue and told me I could stay if I would pull to the back of the building. I appreciated his mercy, but it was difficult to go back to sleep after being awakened.

Tuesday was a long day of driving that ended at the Pilot in Bloomington, Illinois. The Pilot was packed to the gills, but we luckily secured a spot and I got a glorious shower. Bloomington is adjacent to Normal, Illinois and is the proud home of the snack food, Beer Nuts. The Beer Nuts company is still family owned, and Bloomington remains the only production site.[77]

On Wednesday morning, a thick blanket of fog helped to make locating the customer in Romeoville a unique adventure. If not for calling to confirm the directions, I might never have found them.

After delivery, we picked up another load in Bolingbrook, just four miles away, which delivered to Topeka, Kansas. We ran all day and made it to the Kansas City terminal for the night. I performed some minor faith healing on my logbook, but I kept it looking legal. Necessity dictates that rules sometimes be bent, although I have yet to bend them beyond the point of feasible repair. I hate telling little white lies, so I avoid putting myself in a position where I have to whenever possible. Nevertheless, the rigid inflexibility of DOT regulations makes it impossible for a driver to never be forced into logbook creativity. While I do not endorse lying on a logbook, inflexible rules for an unpredictable job set the stage for unavoidable moral conundrums.

Thursday was a crazy day. It started out okay—the delivery to Target in Topeka went fine. Afterward, I had an array of beaten up empty trailers from which to choose. All of them, except one, had at least one bald tire. The one with no bald tires was missing a mud flap. An AWOL mud flap is not as bad as a bald tire, but it still invites a ticket at a weigh station. Choosing the lesser of the evils, I decided to take my chances on "One Flap." We went to Hill's Pet in Topeka for the next load; the same place we had gone during my first solo week.

The Shipping Department at Hill's Pet told me this would be a live load, but offered to load it on a newer trailer if I preferred.

"Heck yeah!" I exclaimed. This would rid me of "One Flap."

As I waited to be loaded, I got out for a visual inspection of my tractor. I noticed that one of the steer tires was going bald in a couple of places. It looked bad enough that I called the company Breakdown Department, and they told me to go to Cross Midwest Tire in Topeka to have it replaced. They added that I should tell Cross Midwest to use the spare tire on the back of the cab.

When I arrived at Cross Midwest, the technician pointed out that my spare tire was a recap, and it is against DOT regulations to have a recap as a steer tire. I called Breakdown again and they reluctantly agreed to buy me a new one. I was confused by the reluctance because I sure as heck wasn't going anywhere without one.

After getting my new tire, I returned to Hill's Pet to find that my trailer still was not loaded. I went in to talk to Shipping, and they told me it was loaded on the original trailer I'd brought in.

Fabulous! I'm stuck with "One Flap" again.

Pet food is always a heavy load, and it is imperative to get it weighed as soon as possible to ensure a legal weight. The only nearby place to weigh was at the city scales, just down the road from Hill's. After waiting there for what seemed an eternity, the "Weighmaster," who was attired in a pair of Boy Scout shorts, arrived on a bicycle. It brought surreal closure to a crazy day.

We went to a truck stop in Maple Hill, Kansas where I purchased a new mud flap and replaced it myself. The temperature was dropping rapidly and, by the time I got the flap on, I could no longer feel my hands.

Friday was a ball breaker! Once again, I had to bend the rules to make my appointment in Aurora, Colorado. We then zipped to Ft. Lupton, Colorado to pick up a load going to Hoosick Falls, New York. I was happy to get a good run, but this one would test my ability to conserve my remaining logbook hours. I would be as dry as the Sahara for hours by the time I got to Hoosick

Falls. However, my hours were tight because of a superb week—around 3200 miles.

We drove 670 miles on Saturday and ended up in Brooklyn, Iowa. Brooklyn is a small rural town known as the *Community of Flags*. Brooklyn's permanent display of flags features an enormous American flag on an 80-foot pole. The flags from all fifty states, all branches of the Armed Services, and different special interest and international flags surround the gigantic flag. Brooklyn's downtown streets are lined with flags of various countries.[78]

After doing the math for my trip to Hoosick Falls, I realized I'd be cutting it even closer than I'd previously thought. Spending the night in the Community of Flags might turn out to be a source of irony. The Hoosick Falls run just might leave my butt flapping in the breeze.

Week 48: Imprisoned Kitty and Grandma Moses

We got to a rest area just west of Kingsville, Ohio on Sunday, which marked three consecutive days of over six hundred miles. Management of my remaining hours was going to be tighter than spandex on a Sumo wrestler, but it just might be possible to do it within legal boundaries…barely.

We left at midnight on Monday, and we made to the customer in Hoosick Falls both on time and legally; before I promptly locked my keys in the truck. I feared this eventually happening, and I kicked myself for procrastinating on getting a spare key made. I peered into the truck helplessly while Kitty sat locked inside, meowing happily as if nothing were wrong. I cursed the Gods for failing to endow her with the intellect, the strength, or the fingers to open the door.

I walked inside the customer's building and sheepishly approached a woman sitting behind a desk in the Receiving Department.

"I have a delivery for you, but I've locked my keys in the truck," I announced with embarrassment.

As she called a locksmith, I remembered a trick Brian showed me. While I won't describe, in detail, the method of breaking into a Freightliner, a strategically placed coat hanger—and a lot of luck—will pop the door right open. I had nothing to lose, so I found a coat hanger and tried it. As I fumbled and probed, Kitty watched with curiosity, oblivious to her imprisonment. After a few minutes of clumsy probing, I hit the sweet spot and the door popped open. I heaved a sigh of relief and thanked the woman whose attempts to find a locksmith had failed.

With the crisis behind me, I began to admire the beauty of this quaint little town. A gentle breeze swept through a wooded area behind the building, and a temperature of 68 degrees belied the typical harshness of upstate New York weather in

November. Earlier, as I drove through the heart of picturesque Hoosick Falls, it struck me as a perfect setting for an artist. I later discovered that it was.

The artwork of Grandma Moses was first discovered in the window of Thorpe's drugstore in Hoosick Falls.[79] She is now buried beside her husband on a hill in Maple Grove Cemetery, overlooking the town she loved.

With my keys clutched firmly in my hand and a smile inspired by the lovely setting, my spirits soared as I climbed into the truck to back into the dock. When I was halfway to the dock, the low-level air alarm screamed a deafening and continuous tone. A few seconds later, the trailer spring brakes engaged. When air pressure goes below 90psi, it triggers the low-level air alarm. If it drops below 60psi, a fail-safe mechanism causes the trailer spring brakes to engage. With my brief moment of bliss rudely interrupted, I was back to a cold, hard reality of trucking: Shit happens when you least expect it!

The truck was not going to budge until the air pressure was back up. I tried every trick I knew, but the air pressure was down for the count. My hoses were intact, so I assumed the compressor had died. By this time, I was on a first name basis with the company Breakdown Department.

I made another uncomfortable march into the Receiving Department.

"You're not going to believe this," I announced with chagrin, "but I think my air compressor died, and I'm stuck in your docking area until road service gets here."

"This just isn't your day," smiled the woman from behind the desk.

An hour and a half later, a service truck arrived. Kitty immediately jumped to the driver's windowsill to investigate the mechanic. As luck would have it, the mechanic was a cat lover too, so we talked about cats while he worked.

The air compressor was fine. He said the air dryer kept purging and needed a new valve. He fixed it in about five minutes after identifying the problem. Despite the back-to-back disasters, the beautiful weather, friendly conversation, and lovely setting lifted my spirits again. For the first time, maybe ever, I understood that attitude is a state of mind rather than a result of events.

An equally profound truth was that my logbook had no hours remaining. I called dispatch to tell them I'd be doing a 34-hour restart. After delivering and thanking the Receiving Department for their patience and understanding, we went to a small truck stop in Ballston Lake, New York. I called Brian to tell him about my day and thank him for showing me the door-opening trick.

"It really saved my ass today!" I assured him.

A pub was next to the truck stop, and I instinctively felt that a Guinness with my name on it waited inside, especially since I wasn't driving tomorrow. A light rain had invaded this beautiful day, but it failed to dampen my spirits as I trudged to the bar, enjoying the music of the raindrops bouncing off my umbrella. I was happy and proud to have weathered today's storm with a smile.

I spent the next day walking around Ballston Lake and watching movies in the truck. The rain had subsided, leaving the weather balmy and in the high 50's.

On Wednesday, dispatch gave me two pre-planned loads designed to get me home on Monday. We picked up the first one in Fort Edwards, New York. Heavy construction impeded the drop lot, making it hard to maneuver the empty trailer into a slot. A year ago, precision maneuvering like that would have caused me to soil my pants.

After picking up the load, I decided to make it a short day. We spent the night in a service area ninety miles north of New York City. For the first time ever, I tried a famous Nathan's hot dog. It wasn't bad, but I didn't see cause for a fuss. I guess I wasn't accustomed to hearing my hot dog go "snap" when I bit into it.

South Boston, Virginia was the next destination, home of the "I ain't got no quarters" cashier. We left at 1am after my unsuccessful attempt to sleep. It rained all day with an intensity that can aptly be called a "frog strangler." Every time I needed to watch for a road sign, it poured even more vigorously. The mad rainstorm exacerbated the congestion through Baltimore and around Washington, D.C., slowing traffic to a wheezing crawl. Nonetheless, we made it to South Boston where my favorite cashier was absent this time. I could not resist another indulgence of Bojangle's chicken and, afterward, I slept like a baby.

The delivery to Dollar General the next morning went fine, and then we picked up the next load in Richmond. Like Dollar General, the shipper in Richmond was slow, but the rain had stopped and a lovely day began to blossom. This load delivered to Anniston, Alabama Sunday evening, and then we'd be homeward bound. After loading in Richmond, we spent the night in Salisbury, North Carolina.

Salisbury is home to famed North Carolina soft drink, Cheerwine. The Carolina Beverage Corporation of Salisbury has produced Cheerwine since 1917. Cheerwine is unusual among sodas for what the company calls "its cherry taste and rich burgundy color."[80] I tried a Cheerwine in Salisbury, and I'll admit to its unique blend.

We arrived in Tallapoosa, Georgia on Saturday afternoon. We were only thirty-eight miles away from tomorrow evening's delivery. I planned to stay up as late as I wanted and then sleep with impunity. I relished the idea of not setting the alarm.

Detour: The Image of Truckers

If we are to believe the stereotypical image painted by Hollywood, the average trucker is an uneducated, unkempt redneck who never quite mastered the art of taking a shower. Movies such as the Stephen Spielberg classic *Duel*, Stephen King's *Maximum Overdrive*, and *Jeepers Creepers* go so far as to make truckers look like psychopathic murderers. A more recent Lifetime movie, *Big Driver*, based on a Stephen King short story portrays a trucker as a brutal rapist. Although I remain a Stephen King fan, his work certainly goes a long way toward casting the image of truckers back into the Stone Age. The typical Hollywood trucker wears an old stained baseball cap, adorns his ample midsection with plenty of flannel, hits on every woman he sees while hiding his wedding ring, and answers to a name such as Cletus, Earl, or Scooter.

Not to single out Mr. King, but it would be nice if a writer of his stature and influence would portray a fictional trucker as the vast majority of us <u>really</u> are: hardworking and honest men and women who leave their families behind for days and weeks to deliver freight across the country.

Sadly, however, the formulation of any stereotype commonly stems from a small kernel of truth. I see plenty of unshaven drivers with, perhaps, a streak of fifth-wheel grease on their tee shirt and splotches of mud here and there. I am occasionally one of those individuals myself. The nature of the work is not glamorous, and it is often impossible to avoid falling victim to unkemptness.

Even so, a handful of drivers take it a step further and serve as embarrassing ambassadors to the industry. Once, at a truck stop in Tallapoosa, Georgia, I watched a dirty and ragged-looking man approach my truck. I considered crawling into the sleeper berth to avoid a vagrant's appeal for money. However, as he came closer, I discerned a company logo on his tattered cap—he was a driver!

Truckers are not known as fashion plates nor, should they be. I, for one, dress for comfort on the road and do not attempt to impress Mr. Blackwell. Nonetheless, when a driver gets to the point where he is indistinguishable from a beggar, perhaps it is time for him to reevaluate his personal grooming habits.

In reality, the majority of truckers do not fit the stereotypical image. Most truckers are easy-going, good-hearted people, and they are more educated than many might think. According to a profile in *Newport Communications*, about half of truckers have some college education, and approximately 90% have a high school diploma or equivalent.

Truck drivers come from all walks of life, and plenty of college graduates drive trucks. Doctors, lawyers, nurses, police officers, CPA's, and even members of MENSA are current or former truck drivers. Former Colorado U.S. Senate Representative, Ben Nighthorse Campbell was also a truck driver. Through trucking, Mr. Campbell financed his college education and earned his degree from San Jose State University. This former trucker also competed in the 1964 Olympics as a member of the U.S. Judo team. Other famous names of erstwhile truck drivers include Chevy Chase, James Cameron, Viggo Mortensen, Richard Pryor, Charles Bronson, Liam Neeson, Sean Connery, and Elvis Presley. The future "King" drove for the aptly named Crown Electric Company. A musician for whom a young Presley auditioned advised him: "Stick to driving a truck, because you'll never make it as a singer."[81]

Misunderstanding and lack of education on the part of the motoring public also contribute to the negative image of truckers. A common complaint pertains to truckers "riding beside each other" and preventing four-wheelers from passing. The public may not be aware that most major trucking companies govern their trucks to have top speeds of 65mph or less. Because of this, trucks are often stuck beside one another longer than they would like to be. This is just as frustrating to the trucker attempting to pass as to the cars stuck behind him.

Another complaint is: "Why do you truckers put your turn signal on right when I get beside you?"

Professional truck drivers look ahead for long distances to see potential hazards or slow-moving traffic. Many times, they are asking you to either hurry up or to back off, especially if you have been riding alongside for a while. We do not think we own the road; we are just asking you to work with us.[82]

A complaint fired directly at me by an angry four-wheeler was, "Why did you wait until I got in the right lane to pass you, and then decide to move over?"

First, the right lane is not for passing. Passing a big truck on the right is never a good idea. Second, trucks have to give ample passing room to the vehicle they are passing before moving back into the right lane. Imagine if all truckers drove like cars—swerving between lanes like a demon. With patience, everybody wins!

In the glory days of trucking, truckers were the Knights of the Road, always willing to help a motorist in distress. When the lyrical stories of C.W. McCall permeated the radio airwaves in the 1970's and *Smokey and the Bandit* cast truckers in a heroic light, young boys euphorically pumped their arms when a mighty diesel passed.

Nowadays, that image is tarnished at best, and there is no single answer to explain it. One explanation lies in the explosion of traffic volume in the last few years. It is impossible to know if someone really needs help when so many cars and trucks pull onto the shoulder. In addition, insurance regulations that did not exist in the "glory days" now prevent truckers from picking up a motorist no matter what the circumstances. Truckers are dollar signs to lawyers, and if we pick someone up and then have an accident, our career is over, and possibly our freedom as well. It is a sad fact that a good deed is often too great a risk to our own well-being <u>and</u> to the loads we are hauling.

There are also many ways that truckers exacerbate their own negative image. A lack of basic personal grooming is one of the worst culprits. No one expects a trucker to look like a CEO, but it isn't asking much to expect him to shower regularly, brush his teeth, and throw on a fresh pair of clothing every couple of days. Most truckers do maintain an acceptable level of hygiene, but they aren't the ones remembered by the general public.

Turning on the CB radio is almost certain to formulate a negative image of truckers. The excessive use of profanity, threats, bigotry, gay bashing, womanizing, and general ignorance makes truckers appear as ill-bred knuckle draggers. The drivers who do not act that way generally do not participate in those conversations. Thus, it seems to the casual listener that *all truckers* are like that. I have made little mention of the CB radio in this chronicle, and the reason is simple; my CB remains off at least 95% of the time. I know many drivers who share in this practice. I'm not sure that truckers will ever decide to clean up the airwaves but, until that time, the On/Off switch provides a viable alternative.

The condition of many truck stops also illuminates truckers in a negative light. Some truck stops literally smell like a urinal. While a large part of truck stop cleanliness responsibility falls upon the facility management, drivers need to bear their share as well. There is no reason for a driver to haphazardly discard trash and pee bottles at a truck stop. This is absolutely disgusting, and I make no excuse for the drivers who are too lazy to walk to the trashcan. I would like to see truck stops impose a stiff penalty to any driver caught throwing a pee bottle anywhere besides a waste receptacle. On the same note, truck stops need to be better at removing waste on a regular schedule. Nothing is more sickening than to walk across the parking lot when the wind wafts an odor of rotting food and urine directly into your face.

There are things that both truckers and the motoring public can do for an image makeover. Truckers should pay heed to personal hygiene and appearance. We don't need to dress for an opera opening, but our appearance (and fragrance) should not be offensive. We are the professional drivers, and we should act accordingly. Stop tailgating, stop speeding through construction zones and do not bully four-wheelers. Those who are unable to share the road with professionalism and respect should not be behind the wheel of a 40-ton vehicle.

Dispose of trash in the proper place. Enough said!

Finally, treating waitresses and cashiers with respect, presenting ourselves to customers and shippers in a professional manner, and cleaning up our filthy mouths on the CB would go a long way toward improving our image.

The motoring public could also use an education on sharing the road with trucks. A simple understanding of what trucks can (and cannot) do would alleviate plenty of road rage and middle fingers. Please remind yourself that the trucks annoying you are the main reason you enjoy the comfort and standard of living that you have. Point to anything you own, and know that a truck delivered it to the place you got it.

Trucks and truckers are here to stay. Our public perception lies largely in our own hands.

Week 49 and 50: Searching for Elvis

We arrived in Anniston over an hour early and were in the dock by 9pm. It took a mere three and a half hours after that for the leisurely lumpers to unload the truck. It was after 3am when we got home.

I stayed home three days longer than planned due to a horrible crick in my neck, for which I went to a chiropractor three times. I could barely lift a cup of coffee with my right arm, much less shift the gears in a big rig.

After a week at home, I still did not have a full range of motion in my right arm. The pain was still intense, but I sucked it up and hit the road anyway. Truckers do not get sick days, and I needed to get back on the road if I wanted to make any money.

We left on Monday, and the searing pain that shot from my arm to my neck the first time I shifted gears almost made me shut the truck off and go back to the house. After rubbing an ungodly amount of Tiger Balm on my neck and shoulder and taking a couple of Naproxen tablets, the pain dulled... just a little.

We picked up our initial load in Muscle Shoals, Alabama. Muscle Shoals is probably one of the world's most unassuming "music capitals" because of remaining unspoiled by the music industry. FAME Studios has made a staggering contribution to American popular music from the 1960's up to today. Many artists have gone to Muscle Shoals in order to escape the limelight and record their signature works. The list of artists who have recorded in Muscle Shoals reads like a Who's Who of the music industry: Percy Sledge, Eric Clapton, Lynyrd Skynyrd, The Allman Brothers, Cher, Jimmy Buffet, Joe Cocker, Jerry Lee Lewis, The Rolling Stones, and Carrie Underwood... just to name a few. [83]

At the Muscle Shoals shipper, I had to blindside into a dock around another truck. This time, I did it with so much grace and ease that another driver commented that I'd made it look easy.

My neck and shoulder were still giving me fits, but the compliment made me forget about the pain for a moment.

This load would be going to Pratt, Kansas. After loading, I stopped to weigh at a truck stop in Tuscumbia, Alabama. Tuscumbia is the hometown of Helen Keller and the location of the Alabama Music Hall of Fame.[84] I decided to shut down for the evening in Tuscumbia because it was already getting dark.

We left at 2:30am the next morning and the pain in my neck, shoulder, and arm continued to induce intermittent girlish whimpers from me. I honestly did not know whether I'd make it through this run.

I stopped for fuel at Love's in Morrilton, Arkansas and decided to add some coolant since the level looked a little low. Not thinking, I opened the coolant reservoir cap too fast and was deluged with a hot coolant shower. The blunder also caused the cap to become a projectile. As I recovered from my coolant bath, I realized the cap could have spewed just about anywhere. I searched for a few minutes but could not find it anywhere. After confirming the truck stop did not have a replacement cap, I spotted an auto parts store across the road. In a long shot, I walked over to see if they had a cap that would fit a Freightliner...they didn't. I returned to the truck, preparing to cap the reservoir with a rag and duct tape to get me to the next truck stop when I happened to see the cap neatly lodged between two hoses. I breathed a sigh of relief, but this little adventure had cost me almost an hour.

We made it to Billings, Oklahoma for the night without further incident. As I prepared the evening meal, I noted that my muscles were losing tone. I am unable to exercise while my neck and shoulder are dysfunctional, and I have no idea how long I'll be riding the pine on the sidelines.

The delivery to Pratt went smoothly. Called the *Gateway to the High Plains*, the area surrounding Pratt, Kansas is a rolling plain of green grassland, broken by the Ninnescah River and the hills along Elm and Turkey creeks. What began as a practical joke is now one of Pratt's unique features.[85] There are two water towers in the town, one painted with the word "Hot" and the other, "Cold".

The frosty morning air in Pratt took me by surprise. When I stepped out of the truck, it quickly became apparent that sandals were inappropriate footwear. After changing into something more appropriate, we went to Salina, Kansas for the next load.

Salina was home to the "Last Great Aviation Record" when world-renowned adventurer Steve Fossett took off from the Salina airport in the Virgin Atlantic Global Flyer to attempt the first solo, non-stop, non-refueled trip around the world by airplane. Fossett completed the record-breaking flight on March 3, 2005 when he landed back at the Salina airport sixty-seven hours, one minute, and ten seconds later.[86]

At the Salina shipper, I somehow managed to run the tractor's fifth wheel past the trailer kingpin again. I corrected the problem this time, but I was annoyed at myself for making this dumb mistake again.

We got our first taste of snow this winter as we approached Topeka, and then we got a veritable mouthful. Snow, sleet, and ice hammered us with the hat trick of winter *yuck*. It took almost two hours to crawl through an icy Kansas City rush hour, but we made it to the terminal safely.

I was exhausted when we arrived and I had fallen woefully behind on my paperwork. As I prepared for the awaiting drudgery, Kitty jumped in the driver's seat and promptly puked in the driver's door storage pocket, all over my steel measuring tape and permit book. It took forever to fish paper towels in and out of the small pocket to absorb the massive amount of Kitty vomit. I just wanted this day to end!

We woke up to more ice and freezing rain, and the conditions remained unchanged for most of the morning. I almost got stuck on a sheet of ice as I exited the fuel island at a truck stop in Higginsville, Missouri. It makes me mad enough to chew nails when truck stops are too cheap and/or lazy to salt their lots in icy conditions.

The mercury in the thermometer began to rise a little when we got south of St. Louis, and the freezing rain became regular rain. We were then doomed to get "regularly" rained on for the remainder of the day. The damp weather exacerbated the pain in my ailing neck and shoulder, and I was in a foul mood by the time we reached Hayti, Missouri for the night. My malady gave rise to concern as it forced me to brace my right arm with my left in the shower in order to shave.

We delivered to Memphis the next morning with no problems. We traveled down Elvis Presley Boulevard to get to the shipper for our next load. I called Brian to tell him that I had (sort of) found Elvis.

Eveready Battery in Memphis was crowded and tight, and docking promised to be a barrel of laughs. At 1pm, some of the drivers who had been sitting in the dock since daybreak were getting downright irate. This is, usually, a bad idea because becoming indignant with a shipper often inspires them to make the driver wait even longer. In extreme cases, drivers are asked to leave without their load. I, typically, play a computer game, read, or just go to sleep when faced with the prospect of sitting in the dock for a long stretch.

We were loaded by 2pm and made it to Ozora, Missouri for the night. This load was headed to Fridley, Minnesota—a perfect winter destination! If I had known what was in store for me in Fridley, I might have never left Ozora.

The roads in Illinois were icy and terrible the next day. Big trucks and four-wheelers spilled along the median and shoulder like a demolition derby. To make matters worse, dispatch changed my delivery appointment from Monday morning to Sunday night. This meant that I would have to find a place to park in the Minneapolis/St. Paul area in the middle of the night—not an attractive prospect.

I called Dick to complain about my appointment time being changed, arguing that this was not the load I accepted. To my utter astonishment, Dick offered to change it back. Because of his uncharacteristic display of quasi humanity, I agreed to go ahead and deliver it on Sunday night. It went against my better judgment, but my system remained short-circuited by the shocking exhibit of understanding from Dick. I did not know if I'd awakened in an alternate universe, but I hoped I had a beach house, a new Ford pickup, and a fat bank account if that were the case.

When we stopped at the terminal in Ottawa, Illinois for fuel, the Ice Capades could have been held in the terminal parking lot. After fueling, I had to detour through the city because of a big truck stuck in the snow on my exit ramp. To add to the misery, the sun came out long enough to melt the condensation that had formed and frozen inside the truck. While desperately trying to avoid being stuck in icy Ottawa, I literally had to weather a rainstorm inside the truck.

We made it to the TA in Janesville, Wisconsin where I was relieved to get through the day intact. I considered a snowy trek across the road to the movie theater but decided I'd had enough drama for one day.

Week 51: Frigid in Fridley

We left Janesville at 11:30am and the road conditions improved as we made our way through Wisconsin toward Minnesota. It was already dark when we arrived at the Target in Fridley, and the shockingly cold weather made me gasp when I opened the door. I napped in the truck during the four hours it took to be unloaded.

It was approaching midnight as we left Target to search for a parking place in the Minneapolis/St. Paul area. The CVS store where I delivered on my prior trip to Fridley was not far from my current location, so I decided to give it a shot. There were *Private Property* signs all over the place, but there was a large alley behind the shopping center next to CVS.

I went down the alley and made a tight U-turn at the end to point myself back in a more favorable direction. Unfortunately, it was so cold that my plastic air hoses had lost much of their elasticity. When I heard the familiar hiss of escaping air in mid-turn, I wasn't sure which was deflating faster—the air pressure or my resolve. I got out into the assaulting cold to see my red air hose snapped in two. The truck was jackknifed in mid-turn behind the shopping center's liquor store—this sucked!

I knew I'd have to call for someone to replace the hose, but I wanted to move the truck into a less embarrassing position before calling. With duct tape in hand, I embarked on the task of a temporary repair. Remembering a trick I'd heard another driver describe, I found a ballpoint pen inside the truck and unscrewed it. Taking the hollow front end of the pen, I cut off the tip with my knife to produce a sturdy, hollow plastic tube. The ends would fit perfectly into each side of the broken air hose, and then I'd wrap plenty of duct tape around the repair. A perfect temporary solution! Hopefully, the repair would last long enough to allow me to straighten up and get to the curb.

It did not take long to realize that my cumbersome gloves hindered my efforts. The thick, arctic Windstopper gloves would have been perfect if I'd been mushing Siberian huskies in the Iditarod, but not so much for trying to repair an air hose with duct tape. When I removed the gloves, it took about thirty seconds to lose sensation in my fingers. To add to the challenge, I had to do it quickly because the extreme cold caused the sticky side of the tape to freeze before I could wrap it around the hose. Somehow, I finally managed to get enough tape wrapped around the tubing to get me to the curb.

The road service truck was a welcome sight when it arrived. The thick-blooded Minnesota native braved the intense cold as he replaced the hose, effectively making me feel like a pantywaist. As I put the ordeal behind me and prepared to spend a bone-chilling night in an alley behind a liquor store, I was pretty sure this Southern boy was out of his element in a Minnesota winter.

I took a load offering the next morning to Hunt Valley, Maryland and we picked it up in New Ulm, Minnesota. Located in the triangle of land formed by the gathering of the Minnesota River and the Cottonwood River,[87] New Ulm once billed itself "Polka Capital of the Nation." For years, polka lovers enjoyed New Ulm's annual Polka Days every July. Polka lovers still step and hop their way to New Ulm for the annual Oktoberfest in celebration of the town's German heritage.

Salt, slush, and winter muck covered the truck as we left New Ulm. I got an unexpected call from Rita, Merlin's wife, for the first time in a while. She said that Merlin was starting to act like himself again, but his foot was still bad. It remained unknown when he could return to work or, for that matter, whether he would ever drive a truck again. I wished her and Merlin all the best as we pulled into the Trucker's Inn near Dakota, Minnesota for the night. My ailing neck and shoulder were finally showing signs of improvement. Regrettably, I seemed to have picked up a "Minnesota bug" that prompted me to buy some cold medicine before going to bed.

I had some unpleasant words with a four-wheeler in Ottawa, Illinois the next day for thoughtlessly blocking me in at a truck stop. He finally recognized the error of his ways and moved before I alerted management.

I had planned to go to Ohio, but the Minnesota bug convinced me to call it a day at the last eastbound travel plaza on I-80 in Indiana. I hoped to sleep this nasty little bug out of my system.

We spent Wednesday night at a company terminal in New Kingstown, Pennsylvania and arrived at the customer in Hunt Valley, Maryland at 3am on Thursday. The customer sent me to a warehouse in a different part of town, which is always a pain in the ass. I turned around in the small lot to avoid blindsiding in the dark and nearly jackknifed because the yard was so tiny.

After delivery, the forklift driver gave me directions to a drop yard where I could park. I was grateful, because I had no idea where we'd park at 4am. I found the drop yard, crawled into the sleeper berth, and fell into a sleep of death. I had yet to shake the Minnesota bug, and I felt terrible.

I awoke from my Lazarus sleep at 10am and got a load offering from Carlisle, Pennsylvania to Aiken, South Carolina. Carlisle is famous to many people for its car shows at the Carlisle Fairgrounds.[88] After loading in Carlisle, we made it to Tom's Brook, Virginia for the night.

We delivered in Aiken at 10am the next morning, and then dispatch informed me it would be at least three or four hours before the next load offering. I replied that I would be unable to legally pick up a load in three or four hours, so we went to a truck stop expecting to wait until the next morning for a load. I was shocked when dispatch offered me the option to deadhead three hundred miles to go home. Freight really must have been slow, because a 300-mile deadhead for home time is almost unheard of.

I accepted the home option and with my remaining time, went to Madison, Georgia for the night. In 2001, Holiday Travel magazine named Madison "The Prettiest Small Town in America".[89] The Madison truck stop, however, looked just about like all the rest. We left Madison at 2am and arrived home in Scottsboro at 7am on Saturday.

Week 52: Reflections

I still was not feeling great after a few days at home, but the Minnesota bug was finally down to its last buzz. A couple more trips to the chiropractor offered my neck and shoulder continued improvement, but my right arm had yet to regain full strength.

On Wednesday, I reluctantly sent a message to dispatch that I was available for a load offering. We got one from Cherokee, Alabama to Fort Worth, Texas. I was grateful for a Texas run because I did not want to go back north right out of the starting gate.

The directions to the shipper in Cherokee were vague, and no one answered the phone when I attempted to call for more specific ones. We'd just have to wing it! Unlike the bone-rattling temperatures in Minnesota, it was unseasonably warm in Alabama—it felt almost like spring.

The directions to the Cherokee shipper were wrong, but we found the place anyway. The sun was already sinking beneath the horizon by the time we were loaded, so I pulled in front of an abandoned building in Cherokee to spend the night. While there are a few drivers who prefer to run at night, the increased difficulty in finding parking after dark usually deters me when I have a choice. I love to get up early and run before daybreak. Watching the world come to life in the morning has always been my favorite time of day.

The directions to the customer in Fort Worth were also wrong, but I got someone on the phone this time for verbal instructions. I never hesitate to call a customer or shipper for directions if need be, because engaging in a wild goose chase in a big truck is not my idea of fun.

We went to the company terminal in Wilmer, Texas before noon, and the beautiful Alabama weather had followed us to Texas. It remained in the low to mid-70's all day.

The delivery to Fort Worth went perfectly, but the next load offering was a choice between New York City and Newark, New Jersey with a stop-off. That is like a choice between getting your hand slammed in the door of a Plymouth Duster and getting it slammed in the door of a Dodge Dart. Despite the stop-off, I took the New Jersey run—I wanted no part of New York City.

We picked up the New Jersey load in Ennis, Texas. Ennis has the widest main street in America because it is actually two separate streets, each on opposite sides of the railroad track that runs through town.[90] Not to be outdone by New Ulm, Minnesota, Ennis holds the annual National Polka Festival featuring food, music, dancing, and a parade through downtown. We polkaed our way out of Ennis to the Flying J in Texarkana, Arkansas for the night.

We left Texarkana at 3am Saturday morning and drove to a small truck stop in Crab Orchard, Tennessee. This small town is named for its abundance of wild crab apple trees. Crab Orchard has also given its name to a rare type of durable sandstone found in the area. Numerous buildings, including the Cumberland County Courthouse, are constructed with Crab Orchard stone.[91]

The first full year of my solo-driving career drew to its conclusion in the tiny Tennessee town of Crab Orchard. The small truck stop where we sat offered a dirt lot filled with potholes, but we parked on level ground with a clear view of the city. The dirty and pothole-filled yard of the truck stop was in stark contrast to the beauty of the landscape of this small rural town on the horizon.

Crab Orchard was a perfect metaphor for my first year on the road: potholes and level ground, ugliness and beauty, suffocating and refreshing. Over the past year, I ferried back and forth regarding my decision to change careers. On one day, it was the best decision I ever made; on the next, it was the dumbest thing I've ever done.

As I sat in the truck reflecting on the past year, I realized that the potholes and level ground of Crab Orchard are in the path of everyone, no matter what profession they choose. We all must endure the potholes to marvel at the beauty of the horizon. After a year of being on the road, I was still undecided as to whether I loved or hated trucking, but one thing was for certain—it's one hell of a ride!

Afterword

After taking some time off driving to write this travelogue, I was utterly shocked when I realized that I missed being on the road. As the time rapidly approached to go back out there, another part of me dreaded it with a passion. This dichotomy is indicative of the trucking industry as a whole. As drivers, we have to decide whether the positives outweigh the negatives. For those who think so, trucking can be a rewarding, lifelong career. For those who do not, it will probably be a short career filled with frustration. Trucking certainly has its share of yin and yang.

The negatives of trucking are many: unglamorous and thankless work, being away from home and family, loneliness and high stress, wildly-varying paychecks, traffic, the endless spattering of *No trucks allowed* signs, and the list goes on and on. The trucking industry is ruthless and demanding with a high failure rate and merciless odds. Truck drivers remain among the only labor groups in America exempt from the Fair Labor Standards Act, and many trucking companies continue to treat their drivers as faceless truck numbers rather than human beings. Lawmakers in Washington continue to believe that piling on more and more rules and regulations will make the roads safer when, in reality, they are making the job so undesirable that veterans are leaving the industry in droves. Long weeks away from home, a general lack of respect and consideration from trucking companies and the motoring public and stagnant salaries are even making it difficult to retain rookies in the industry.

A negative image among the motoring public is another cross for the truck driver to bear. In the eyes of many automobile drivers, big trucks are just a nuisance. These are the same people who enjoy slicing into a Christmas ham, or buying a Nintendo for their kids, or just popping into a grocery store for something they want or need. I wonder if these people ever ask themselves, "Where did all this stuff come from?"

The answer is that a truck brought it. Without trucks and their drivers moving freight all over the country, from raw materials to finished products, there would be no Christmas ham, no Nintendo, no stocked grocery store shelves, no fuel at gas stations, no medical supplies at hospitals...or anything else. The standard of living enjoyed by all Americans would decline almost immediately if all truckers decided to unite and shut off their engines. Without the men and women who sacrifice so much to keep the American Dream alive for so many, it would not even be there as a goal to strive toward.

Trucking also has many positive aspects. The absence of a boss hanging over your shoulder is, by far, one of the most attractive features of trucking. The ever-changing scenery of driving across the country makes the prospect of sitting in an office cubicle eight hours a day almost unthinkable. I've heard some veteran drivers say, "Trucking gets in your blood."

I believe that.

I often think about the freight I deliver and how it might make an impact on someone's life. Perhaps the steel beams I delivered to the Mayo Clinic in Jacksonville will provide the foundation for the hospital where a doctor performs life-saving surgery for a child. Perhaps the lumber I delivered to Newnan, Georgia will make up a wall of the new home of a young couple that has worked and saved to realize their dream. As for the thousands of boxes of toilet paper I have delivered all over the country, well...that should darned near earn me a halo!

The negative moniker of truckers and trucking was chiefly bestowed by the uninformed. Trucking is the lifeblood of America, and truckers can take great pride in the service they provide. I can say, without reservation, that I am proud to have been an American Trucker!

Even in a world of satellite maps, GPS systems, Qualcomm messaging, and electronic logs, truckers maintain a bit of the rugged explorer's lifestyle. They are usually far from home and uncertain what lies around the next bend. They are often dirty, tired, and cranky, but when they drive through a dusty rural town and see an eight-year-old boy pumping his arm vigorously and looking up into the cab with wonder and admiration, it seems to be worth it all. Trucking is a tough and rigorous lifestyle, but it is also an escape from the mundane. Despite everything, I'd do it all over again.

Following this first year on the road, Kitty and I would continue to roll across the nation for four more years. Kitty retired from the road at age 15, and I made a brief return to trucking in 2012, only to realize that this lifestyle wasn't for me anymore. In 2008, I met a wonderful woman in El Paso, Texas who, as it turned out, was the love of my life. After enduring a sporadic, long-distance relationship for over a year, I finally moved to El Paso in late 2009. We both eventually decided that we desired a more stable relationship than the road could offer, so I made an eventual exit from trucking.

As of this writing, Kitty is now 17 years old and doing pretty well for an elderly cat. Upon my brief return to trucking in 2012, the now-retired Kitty would meow in anticipation of going on the road when I began to pack up to go out again. I hated not being able to take her but, by this time, she suffered too many senior issues to subject her to life on the road again. She now enjoys her senior years with a family, which includes two dogs, that remains at home. But sometimes, I think a part of Kitty still pines for the road. I think a part of me also does.

In Memoriam

Kitty passed away in July of 2014 about a month shy of her 18th birthday. After having her as a constant companion for the amount of time it would take to raise a child to high school graduation, it was a sad July morning when I reluctantly accepted that July 1, 2014 would be the last day I'd ever spend with her. After suffering multiple senior maladies for the past few years, she had finally cashed in the last of her nine lives.

No less than four times before, I took her to the vet thinking it was the final curtain call but, each time, she fought back with stubborn feline tenacity to once again reign supreme over her two dogs (and two humans) at home. Tonie and I were awed by Kitty's miraculous ability to make a comeback. On that fateful morning, however, it was sadly obvious there would be no amazing recovery this time. Kitty's number had finally been called. As I lifted her lethargic body from her bed and hugged her for one of the last times, she forced a feeble purr, and I recalled one of the first times I'd ever held her like that.

About seventeen years before, I hugged the small and delicate kitten as tightly as I dared as we huddled in the walk-in closet of my one-bedroom apartment among my clothes and next to the water heater. She still had the stitches in her abdomen from recent surgery. I had experimented with different names for the abandoned kitten after I'd claimed her as my own, but none of them seemed to fit, so I just called her "Kitty." By then, she recognized it as her name, so there didn't seem to be a need to change it.

The eerie wail of a tornado warning siren filled the sky in the Five Points Historic District in Huntsville, Alabama. Tornado warnings were nothing new in the Tennessee Valley, but it was impossible to grow accustomed to the foreboding siren that began in a forlorn, low pitch and gradually escalated to an earsplitting high tone that pierced the skull like an icepick. At the verge of insanity, the tone dropped again and the bloodcurdling cycle of horrendous noise began anew.

Just minutes before, I had stepped outside into the humid stillness of the calm before the storm. The sky appeared tinged with a sickly yellow hue as the stifling warm air made it seem difficult to breathe. The sultry air entailed a chilling silence that inspired a sense of dread to anyone familiar with a tornado-prone region. I immediately ran back inside and scooped up Kitty as gently as I could. With no tornado shelter at my apartment complex, Kitty and I went to the only room in the apartment with no windows—the closet.

The power had gone out earlier, so I sat in the inky blackness of the closet expecting to hear the loud, telltale roar similar to a freight train outside, and praying that I wouldn't. Instead, the calming purr of a kitten was the sound that proved to dominate my memory. Kitty's gentle purrs almost made me forget that I was listening for the approach of a tornado as the rhythmic vibrations on my chest resounded serenely and provided calm despite the fearful circumstances. It was the purrs of a three-pound kitten that helped to make me feel safe against the impending danger of a tornado. Who could have known that a little cat had such power?

Over the following seventeen years, Kitty's gentle purrs provided me with needed reassurance in the face of many trials and tribulations. Her ornery feline demeanor supplied me with both laughter and frustration but, as the years passed, our personalities merged into a distinctive understanding and our bond strengthened immeasurably. I did not know a pet could fill my life with such comfort and love before Kitty, and I did not fully recognize the quality of that love until I walked out of the vet's office on that day without her.

As I write this, over six months have gone by since Kitty's passing and, although I still miss her terribly, I am better able to reflect on the memory of her with more joy than sadness. Although I recognize that it is all too easy to attach anthropomorphic characteristics to our pets, especially if they provide a primary source of companionship, it is equally true that, to most of us, pets are much more than "just a dog," or "just a cat." I have no doubt that I'll cherish the memory of Kitty for the rest of my life.

Kitty's purrs, head-butts, cheek rubs, and even scratching provided sanctuary from some of life's harsher realities over the years. Kitty was instrumental in helping me to cope with the death of my Grandmother, the loss of a job and the helpless uncertainty that followed; three horrid winters in upstate New York, an abrupt career change, and too many other personal struggles to name. Kitty remained the only constant in my life during a decade of change, loss, and turmoil.

Finally, she took on the role of shotgun passenger in my eighteen-wheeler. During the five years she traveled across the country with me, she charmed countless security guards at hundreds of freight shippers and customers as we hauled everything from pet food to toilet paper, to Cap'n Crunch to knurled pistons from coast to coast. Her endless curiosity and love of life was never more evident than when she jumped in my lap at the end of a long day to thrust her head out the driver's window and inhale the essence of wherever we happened to be. The pure satisfaction of the gift of life was unmistakable as her eyes glazed over in the bliss of the moment and her little pink nose twitched rapidly, soaking in the aromatic wonders of the world in which we lived. Kitty's ability to draw euphoria out of the act of simply being alive sometimes gave me cause to let go of the day's frustrations and just smile at her contentment. It was but one of the many gifts that Kitty gave me during our time together.

Perhaps the greatest gift from Kitty occurred in the midst of an unlikely love story. When I met Tonie in 2008, she was a college professor in El Paso, Texas and I was a truck driver from Alabama. Despite the disparity of our backgrounds, it was apparent, early on, that we complimented one another like RC Cola and Moon Pie or, in terms of her culture, like Crema and Tacos al pastor. It was an unlikely pairing but, once we'd experienced the magical combination, it was hard to imagine one without the other. Thus began a long-distance relationship that put me on a first-name basis with the American Airlines clerks at the Huntsville International Airport for the next year or so. Finally, we decided it was time for me to move to El Paso, since my job afforded mobility.

Prior to moving to El Paso, the meetings between Tonie and Kitty were cautious. Tonie had never been around cats before, and Kitty was often snobbish toward other humans in general. She was notably persnickety toward human females. Over the years prior to meeting Tonie, my dating life was spread out and erratic, and most of my dates were of the one-and-done variety. But on the rare occasions when I brought a date home, Kitty usually met their intrusion into her court with a challenging glare. I distinctly remember Kitty even giving one of them an aggressive hiss when the lady had the audacity to reach out to pet her. Kitty's history with human females was largely one of antagonism, so both Tonie and I worried about how the scene would play out when I moved to El Paso. Tonie also had two dogs, and Kitty's history with other animals was little better than with humans. So, there was that to worry about too.

The players did not assimilate into the new culture immediately, but Kitty warmed up to the dogs more quickly than we could have imagined, and she warmed up to Tonie even more rapidly. It didn't take long for Tonie to fall in love with Kitty either. Kitty allayed our worst fears by accepting her place into her new extended family with remarkably little fuss. It wasn't long before Kitty began rubbing against Tonie to show her the affection previously reserved exclusively for me. In doing so, perhaps Kitty confirmed that I had finally found the perfect pairing; the RC Cola to my Moon Pie—the Crema to my taco. I could never ask for a greater gift.

Tonie's tears flowed just as freely as mine on the day Kitty died, and it was apparent that we had lost much more than a pet—we had lost a member of the family. Before she died, I kissed her on the top of the head and told her that I loved her, but she already knew that. Despite the pain of losing her, I can take solace in the knowledge that she was loved and cherished. She was my most trusted and welcome companion for the many years before I met Tonie, and she became a treasured member of a new family thereafter. She was undoubtedly one of the well-travelled cats in America, having been through each of the 48 contiguous states, and having left her paws prints in most of them. I could not have asked for a better road companion. She gave me over seventeen years of love and friendship, and I was happy to give it back in return. Tonie and I spread Kitty's ashes beneath a beautiful cottonwood tree on the banks of the Rio Grande so she can forever enjoy the communion with nature that she so adored.

Goodbye my sweet girl. You were so much more than "just a cat." You were the best friend I've ever had.

Rick L. Huffman
January, 2015

About the Author:

Rick L. Huffman began a broadcasting career in 1985 as a part-time disc jockey. Soon making the transition to television, he was involved in every aspect of production over a twenty-year span, which eventually led him to New York. Fed up with high-strung bosses, Rick totally changed gears in 2005 and started driving an 18-wheeler across the country for the next five years.

After making a career change to trucking, it did not take long to see that the story of this unique lifestyle waited to be told. He began taking daily notes on the adventures of road life, intent on telling a story of a passionate group of whom little is known by the general public, namely, truckers.

Rick is a veteran of the United States Navy where he served aboard a submarine during the cold war era. Rick is from Huntsville, Alabama but he now resides in El Paso, Texas.

Upcoming Projects:

The working title of Rick's first novel is: *The Road to Vermont*. On the day after his fiftieth birthday, a lonely long-haul truck driver, Dieter Dietz, wakes up with a hangover in the Mojave Desert near Las Vegas. Having lived a life that he sees as one disaster and disappointment after the next, the recent death of Rue, a twenty-year-old cat who was his closest companion, is simply the latest kick to the groin delivered to him by a pathetic life. Before he retires from trucking and crawls into a whiskey bottle to tolerate the remainder of a miserable existence, he wishes to sprinkle Rue's remains at the corporate headquarters of Ben & Jerry's, since this brand of ice cream was her favorite treat. With the ashes of his beloved cat tucked away in a Prince Albert can, Dieter Dietz meets a host of quirky characters on the road to Vermont who challenge his resignation from life and force him to take an introspective journey inspired both by their own unique lives, and through his own retelling of a hilarious and tragic family history. We are reminded that lives intersect in strange and unpredictable ways and that we never know how our life might make a profound difference in someone else's whether we know about it or not. *The Road to Vermont* is a sweeping, epic tale that takes the reader from the islands of American Samoa, to the fishing docks of small-town Alaska, to the world of the Lucha libre in Mexico City, to the treacherous Appalachian Trail and, of course, across the highways of America.

If you enjoyed this book, please leave a review. It means a lot.

Leave an Amazon review here:
http://www.amazon.com/dp/B00DU0T5SU

Like our Facebook Page:
https://www.facebook.com/pages/American- Trucker/399162519814

Meet Rick and Kitty on YouTube:

Life with Kitty
https://www.youtube.com/watch?v=iP6Xvim79NI

Rick's YouTube Channel
https://www.youtube.com/user/CMVrick/videos

Endnotes

[1] *The Lizard Man of Scape Ore Swamp - RedOrbit* (n.d.). Retrieved from http;//www.redorbit.com/education/reference_library/general-2/cryptozoology/1112948529/lizard-man-of-scape-ore-swamp

[2] *Key Underwood Coon Dog Memorial Graveyard* (n.d.). Retrieved from http://www.coondogcemetery.com

[3] *The Great American Stations – Greenwood, Mississippi* (n.d.). Retrieved from http://www.greatamericanstations.com/Stations/GWD

[4] *Frostproof, Florida – Wikipedia, the free encyclopedia* (n.d.). Retrieved from http://en.wikipedia.org/wiki/Frostproof,_Florida

[5] *City of Vincennes, Indiana – History* (n.d.). Retrieved from http://www.vincennes.org/dev/history/

[6] *Bear Creek, Alabama – Wikipedia, the free encyclopedia* (n.d.). Retrieved from http://en.wikipedia.org/wiki/Bear_Creek,_Alabama

[7] *Welcome to Prosperity, South Carolina - History.* (n.d.). Retrieved from http://www.prosperitysc.com/page/history

[8] *South Carolina, Memories of Swansea – SCIWAY – South Carolina's Information Highway* (n.d.). Retrieved from http://www.sciway.net/hist/swansea-sc-memories.html

[9] *Fort Rucker - Wikipedia, the free encyclopedia.* (n.d.). Retrieved from http://en.wikipedia.org/wiki/Fort_Rucker

[10] *Watch the Latest Promo for the Silver Springs Film Fest!* (n.d.). Retrieved from http://ocalacep.com/cep-news/entry/watch-the-latest-promo-for-the-silver-springs-film-fest

[11] *Celebrate Fitzgerald's 3rd Annual Wild Chicken Festival – WRD News story – Outdoor Central News Network archives* (n.d.). Retrieved from http://www.outdoorcentral.com/mc/pr/03/02/28d4.asp

[12] *Fitzgerald, Georgia: Downtown Wild Chickens – Festival – Roadside America.com* (n.d.). Retrieved from http://www.roadsideamerica.com/tip/14685

[13] *Morristown, Tennessee - Wikipedia, the free encyclopedia.* (n.d.). Retrieved from http://en.wikipedia.org/wiki/Morristown,_Tennessee

[14] *Feisty Females: Alice Harrell Strickland - Diggin' History.* (n.d.). Retrieved from http://historydepot.wordpress.com/2014/08/29/feisty-females-alice-harrell-strickland

[15] *The History of Helena, Montana - Big Sky Fishing.Com.* (n.d.).

Retrieved from http://www.bigskyfishing.com/Montana-Info/helena-mt-2.shtm

[16] *Little Chicago: Cemetery tour a success – North Platte Bulletin* (n.d.). Retrieved from http://www.northplattebulletin.com/index.asp?show=news&action=readStory&storyID=15152&pageID=3

[17] *Ottumwa, Iowa - Wikipedia, the free encyclopedia.* (n.d.). Retrieved from http://en.wikipedia.org/wiki/Ottumwa,_Iowa

[18] *Ogden, Utah - Wikipedia, the free encyclopedia.* (n.d.). Retrieved from http://en.wikipedia.org/wiki/Ogden,_Utah

[19] *Gold Mining in Nevada - Wikipedia, the free encyclopedia.* (n.d.). Retrieved from http://en.wikipedia.org/wiki/Gold_mining_in_Nevada

[20] *Mountain View travel guide - Wikitravel.* (n.d.). Retrieved from http://wikitravel.org/en/Mountain_View_%28California%29

[21] *Interstate 80 - Wyoming - AARoads - The Online Highway Guide!* (n.d.). Retrieved from http://www.aaroads.com/west/i-080_wy.html

[22] *Have a ball at the Testicle Festival - Out West Newspaper.* (n.d.). Retrieved from http://www.outwestnewspaper.com/balls.html

[23] *City of Deland, Florida information.* (n.d.). Retrieved from http://www.delandflorida.com/local/cityinfo.html

[24] *Research on the Health and Wellness of Commercial Truck and Bus Drivers – Summary of an International Conference – Transportation Research Board – Conference Proceedings on the Web 5.* (n.d.). Retrieved from http://onlinepubs.trb.org/onlinepubs/conf/CPW5.pdf

[25] *Truck Drivers Top List of Overweight Workers – HealthDay – News for Healthier Living.* (n.d.). Retrieved from http://consumer.healthday.com/public-health-information-30/economic-status-health-news-224/truck-drivers-secretaries-top-list-of-most-obese-jobs-study-683816.html

[26] *Born And Raised In The South...,: Gadsden, AL.* (n.d.). Retrieved from http://ltc4940.blogspot.com/2009/04/gadston-al.html

[27] *Dacula, Georgia - Wikipedia, the free encyclopedia.* (n.d.). Retrieved from http://en.wikipedia.org/wiki/Dacula,_Georgia

[28] *Historic Dunedin – Dunedin Home of Honeymoon Island* (n.d.). Retrieved from http://www.dunedingov.com/index.aspx?page=2a

[29] *Clinton, Tennessee - Wikipedia, the free encyclopedia.* (n.d.). Retrieved from http://en.wikipedia.org/wiki/Clinton,_Tennessee

[30] *6 Vicious Rivalries — HISTORY Lists.* (n.d.). Retrieved from http://www.history.com/news/history-lists/6-vicious-rivalries

[31] *Green River Gorge|Hiking|Hunting|Fishing|Blue Ridge Mountains ...* (n.d.). Retrieved from http://www.blueridgeheritage.com/attractions-

destinations/green-river-gorge

[32] *AW2010: Friday | Professional Disc Golf Association.* (n.d.). Retrieved from http://www.pdga.com/aw2010-friday

[33] *What is the geography of Sidney, Nebraska? | Answerbag.* (n.d.). Retrieved from http://www.answerbag.com/q_view/215405

[34] *DOWNTOWN SIDNEY MASTER PLAN - Sidney, NE - Official Website.* (n.d.). Retrieved from http://www.cityofsidney.org/index.aspx?NID=359

[35] *Profiles In Desperation | Overdrive - Owner Operators ...* (n.d.). Retrieved from http://www.overdriveonline.com/profiles-in-desperation

[36] *Huntsville, Texas - Wikipedia, the free encyclopedia.* (n.d.). Retrieved from http://en.wikipedia.org/wiki/Huntsville,_Texas

[37] *Best of Brownsville - Tourist Information, Restaurants, Bars ...* (n.d.). Retrieved from http://brownsville.bestoftexas.com/

[38] *What New Mexico town is named for a radio program of the 1940s?* (n.d.). Retrieved from https://answers.yahoo.com/question/index?qid=20070702211758AAo2zxU

[39] *COMMUNITY CONNECTIONS: Volksporters experience Mentone, Pecos ...* (n.d.). Retrieved from http://www.mrt.com/news/opinion/article_eb30900c-7eb2-592a-9b0f-c79a744f2e4a.html

[40] *About Sun Aura Resort* (n.d.). Retrieved from http://www.auraman.com/AuraMan/RESORT_INFO.html

[41] *Findlay, Ohio - Wikipedia, the free encyclopedia.* (n.d.). Retrieved from http://en.wikipedia.org/wiki/Findlay,_Ohio

[42] *Newport, Tennessee - Wikipedia, the free encyclopedia.* (n.d.). Retrieved from http://en.wikipedia.org/wiki/UN/LOCODE%3AUSNPR

[43] *Great Platte River Road Archway Monument - Kearney, Nebraska ...* (n.d.). Retrieved from http://www.city-data.com/articles/Great-Platte-River-Road-Archway-Monument.html

[44] *SevereWeatherWiki - HailTan - Wikispaces.* (n.d.). Retrieved from http://severeweatherwiki.wikispaces.com/HailTan

[45] *The News - Jump Mike Jump.* (n.d.). Retrieved from http://jumpmikejump.org/index.php?option=com_content&view=category&layout=blog&id=1&Itemid=50

[46] : *Niantic, Connecticut - Wikipedia, the free encyclopedia.* (n.d.). Retrieved from http://en.wikipedia.org/wiki/Niantic,_Connecticut

[47] *Baraboo, Wisconsin (WI) Hotels, Homes, and Jobs.* (n.d.). Retrieved from http://www.baraboowisconsin.com

[48] *Winona, Mississippi - Wikipedia, the free encyclopedia.* (n.d.).

Retrieved from http://en.wikipedia.org/wiki/Winona,_Mississippi

[49] *Lake Charles Lakefront Master Plan Follow Up Report.* (n.d.). Retrieved from http://www.cityoflakecharles.com/egov/apps/document/center.egov?vi ew=item&id=737

[50] *Acadiana - Wikipedia, the free encyclopedia.* (n.d.). Retrieved from http://en.wikipedia.org/wiki/Acadiana

[51] *Frank De Vol - Wikipedia, the free encyclopedia.* (n.d.). Retrieved from http://en.wikipedia.org/wiki/Frank_De_Vol

[52] *Wisconsin Amish - WisconsinOutdoor.com.* (n.d.). Retrieved from http://www.wisconsinoutdoor.com/wisconsinamish.htm

[53] *Living in Kalamazoo - The History of Kalamazoo MI.* (n.d.). Retrieved from http://www.kalamazoomi.com/hisf.htm

[54] History - MCHS." *Insert Name of Site in Italics.* N.p., n.d. Web. 8 Sept. 2014 <http://www.mchsociety.org/History.html

[55] *Clarksville, Tennessee - Wikipedia, the free encyclopedia.* (n.d.). Retrieved from http://en.wikipedia.org/wiki/Clarksville,_Tennessee

[56] *WaKeeney.* (n.d.). Retrieved from http://www.wakeeney.org/history-of-wakeeney

[57] *WaKeeney, Kansas - Wikipedia, the free encyclopedia.* (n.d.). Retrieved from http://en.wikipedia.org/wiki/WaKeeney,_Kansas

[58] *McCook, NE | Livable Small Towns | Nebraska Rural Living ...* (n.d.). Retrieved from http*Buffalo Commons Storytelling Festival: Tales and Trails ...* (n.d.). Retrieved from http://www.prairiefirenewspaper.com/2011/05/buffalo-commons-storytelling-festival-tales-and-trails_br://www.nebraskaruralliving.com/towns/mccook.asp

[59]*Vol. 33 No. 1 | January 15, 2001 - Bloustein School.* (n.d.). Retrieved from http://policy.rutgers.edu/faculty/popper/PlainsSense.pdf

[60] *Lawrence, Kansas - Wikipedia, the free encyclopedia.* (n.d.). Retrieved from http://en.wikipedia.org/wiki/Lawrence,_Kansas

[61] *Shelbyville Times Gazette – Moon Pie Festival.* (n.d.). Retrieved from http://www.t-g.com/keywords/moon_pie_festival

[62] *Decatur, Alabama - Wikipedia, the free encyclopedia.* (n.d.). Retrieved from http://en.wikipedia.org/wiki/Decatur,_AL

[63] *The Inquiring Mind: The Demise of the Trucker's Lifestyle.* (n.d.). Retrieved from http://www.theinquiringmind.net/2008/05/demise-of-truckers-lifestyle.html

[64] *Macon Whoopee (CHL) - Wikipedia, the free encyclopedia.* (n.d.). Retrieved from http://en.wikipedia.org/wiki/Macon_Whoopee_(CHL)

[65] *IdleAir - Wikipedia, the free encyclopedia.* (n.d.). Retrieved from

http://en.wikipedia.org/wiki/Idleair

[66] *The Famous Hot Weiner.* (n.d.). Retrieved from http://famoushotweiner.com/index.html

[67] *Flopeye Fish Festival.* (n.d.). Retrieved from http://www.flopeyefishfestival.com/

[68] *What are cheese curds? - FindersFree: What do you want to ...* (n.d.). Retrieved from http://findersfree.com/food-drink-restaurants/cheese-curds

[69] *Forest City, Iowa Colleges, Jobs, Education, Careers ...* (n.d.). Retrieved from http://iowa.careers.org/forest-city

[70] *Welcome to the World's Largest Truckstop – I-80 Exit 284, Walcott, Iowa.* Retrieved from http://iowa80truckstop.com

[71] *Rita Crundwell pleads guilty to embezzling $53M in municipal ...* (n.d.). Retrieved from http://news.nationalpost.com/2012/11/14/small-town-bookkeeper-pleads-guilty-to-embezzling-53m-in-municipal-funds-to-support-lavish-lifestyle

[72] : *Kewanee, Illinois - Wikipedia, the free encyclopedia.* (n.d.). Retrieved from http://en.wikipedia.org/wiki/Kewanee,_Illinois

[73] *Frank P Johnson Speech - Kewanee.* (n.d.). Retrieved from http://kewaneehogdays.com/frank_p_johnson_speech.htm

[74] *What a Wonderful World!: I must go to Toad Suck...* (n.d.). Retrieved from http://uuchild.blogspot.com/2007/04/i-must-go-to-toad-suck.html

[75] *Sallisaw History - www.sallisawchamber.com - Home.* (n.d.). Retrieved from http://www.sallisawchamber.com/history.html

[76] *Sallisaw, OK - Official Website - About Us.* (n.d.). Retrieved from http://www.sallisawok.org/index.aspx?NID=31

[77] *Beer Nuts - Our Story.* (n.d.). Retrieved from http://www.beernuts.com/info/our-story

[78] *Brooklyn, Iowa – Community of Flags - Welcome.* (n.d.). Retrieved from http://www.brooklyniowa.com/

[79] *Walking event announcements in NY, NJ, Delaware, PA.* (n.d.). Retrieved from https://groups.yahoo.com/group/walkatlantic/messages/600?m=s&l=1

[80] *Cheerwine - Wikipedia, the free encyclopedia.* (n.d.). Retrieved from http://en.wikipedia.org/wiki/Cheerwine

[81] *snopes.com: Elvis Presley Told to Stick to Truck Driving.* (n.d.). Retrieved from http://www.snopes.com/music/artists/presley2.asp

[82] *Hey Trucker, Why Do You Do That? - TruckersReport.* (n.d.). Retrieved

from http://www.thetruckersreport.com/why-do-you-do-that-trucker

[83] *Fame Studios – Our History.* Retrieved from http://www.fame2.com/our-history/

[84] *Tuscumbia, Alabama - Simple English Wikipedia, the free* ... (n.d.). Retrieved from http://simple.wikipedia.org/wiki/Tuscumbia,_Alabama

[85] *Pratt Chamber of Commerce - Pratt Has Something for You* ... (n.d.). Retrieved from http://www.prattkansas.org

[86] *Information About Salina, Kansas - ActiveRain.* (n.d.). Retrieved from http://activerain.trulia.com/blogsview/79707/information-about-salina--kansas

[87] *Map of New Ulm MN | MapQuest.com - MapQuest Maps - Driving* ... (n.d.). Retrieved from http://www.mapquest.com/us/mn/new-ulm

[88] Carlisle, Pennsylvania - Wikipedia, the free encyclopedia., n.d. Retrieved from http://en.wikipedia.org/wiki/Carlisle,_PA

[89] Madison, Georgia - Wikipedia, the free encyclopedia., n.d. Retrieved from http://en.wikipedia.org/wiki/Madison,_Georgia

[90] *YOU GO LIVE IN UTAH: April 2008 - blogspot.com.* (n.d.). Retrieved from http://yougoliveinutah.blogspot.com/2008_04_01_archive.html

[91] *Born And Raised In The South...,: Crab Orchard, TN.* (n.d.). Retrieved from http://ltc4940.blogspot.com/2013/02/crab-orchard-tn.html

39082921R00135

Made in the USA
Columbia, SC
08 December 2018